CHINESE IN THE MARKETPLACE
Learn Chinese from advertising

Semmi Brown

Greenwood Press

GREENWOOD PRESS
47 Pokfulam Road, Basement, Hong Kong.
Telephone: 2546 8212

© *Greenwood Press 1996*
All rights reserved. No part of this publication may be reproduced, stored in a retrieval system, or transmitted in any form or by any means – electronic, mechanical, photocopying, or otherwise – without the prior permission of the copyright owner.

First published April, 1996.

ISBN 962-279-173-5

PRINTED IN HONG KONG BY
NGAI SHING PRINTING CO.

PREFACE

This book is written for those who wish to learn Chinese from a "real life" setting.

The book has a number of unique features:

- exercises based on authentic advertisements;
- materials designed for beginners without any prior knowledge of Chinese and, at the same time, for more advanced learners as well, when learning Chinese through "real life" materials;
- each chapter building upon themes and knowledge introduced earlier in the book;
- materials useful for individual study and also for those who work in pairs or small groups or in a larger classroom setting;
- each chapter providing ample opportunity for guided writing activities;
- an "Activities Section" containing a number of exercises designed to reinforce learning and increase enjoyment;
- the use of three different romanisation schemes: Pinyin for those learning Putonghua (Mandarin) and the popular Yale and Lau schemes appropriate for students of Cantonese.

After working through this book, the reader will be familiar with and able to use a number of Chinese phrases and structures.

In addition to these features, this book can be used in conjunction with and is complementary to my earlier work "Read and Write Chinese" (Greenwood Press, 1994).

The advertisements used throughout are taken from authentic copy, much of which has been published in various Hong Kong magazines.

The learning process should be enjoyable and thus more effective: once something has been learned it should remain with the learner more strongly than might otherwise be the case.

I have had a lot of fun and gained a real sense of achievement when writing this book. I hope the reader will also share these feelings when working through the chapters.

Semmi Brown
March, 1996.

ACKNOWLEDGEMENT

No book is so easy to write that the author does not need a little help every now and then during the writing process. This one could not have been made possible without the aid of a number of people: I would like to thank Ms. Leung Yin Bing for her help with the various forms of romanisation, my publisher, Mr. André Loo, for his enthusiasm and numerous helpful suggestions, and my husband, Bob, for his help in proofreading and forebearance.

My thanks also go to the various companies whose advertisements are found within this work. Without their inventiveness and constant search for novelty it would not have been possible to make the book as interesting and varied as it now is.

The author and the publisher wish to thank those companies who have kindly made their advertising copy available for use in this book.

Every effort has been made to trace copyright but in the event of any accidental infringement where copyright has proved untraceable, we shall be pleased to come to a suitable arrangement with the rightful owner.

CONTENTS

Introduction to Chinese Writing		i
The Putonghua Sounds and Tones		ix
The Cantonese Sounds and Tones		xiii
1.	Triangular Relationships	2
2.	Double Happiness	6
3.	Sour, sweet, bitter, hot	14
4.	Mother wants me to learn piano	20
5.	Are you too thin?	27
6.	The head	34
7.	Catch the minutes and seconds	39
8.	Mid-autumn festival	44
9.	Merry Christmas	50
10.	Ordering food	56
11.	From the ocean to the sky	62
12.	Who comes to care about me?	69
13.	You only need a stamp	74
14.	Long, small and easy	81
15.	We never treat anybody equally	88
16.	Yellow pages	93
17.	What kind of things?	101
18.	Fill in the form	109
Activity Sheet		114
Answers		118
Vocabulary List		122
Simplified Vocabulary List		135

INTRODUCTION TO CHINESE WRITING

History

According to ancient Chinese history, there was a clever man named 蒼頡 (cāng jié, chòng git[1]/chong git[3]). He was inspired by the shape of various animals foot prints in the forest and invented the words to correspond with the animals' foot prints. Another version relating the invention of Chinese words is that different tribes had already established some of the simplied "words" or symbols for their own information exchange. 蒼頡 perhaps made a great effort to process and tidy up those symbols, thus forming the very earliest version of Chinese words. Most people at that time presumably found the new system of forming words reasonable and thus were happy to adopt them.

The earliest Chinese symbols we know about were engraved on bones and tortoise shells about 3500 years ago. Over the thousands of years since then, these simple pictures have changed and many more symbols have been added. About 2000 years ago, the Chinese began writing with brushes on paper and silk.

The development of some of the picture characters can be shown from the following table:

3500 years ago to nowadays	Simplified form
sun	
moon	
man	
water	
fire	
eye	
horse	

Chinese characters have been developed and used for more than two thousand years when the scholar, Hui San (許慎), induced six ways of creating Chinese words. Four were used to explain the creation of characters and two described their usage. The four primary methods are as follows:

1. 象形 (xiàng xíng)* (jeuhng yìhng/jeung⁶ ying⁴)
   "Image shapes", or so called "picture characters." The characters describe real objects making words such as sun and moon; mountain and water.

   ☉ = 日   ☽ = 月
   ⛰ = 山   ⋮⋮ = 水

2. 指事 (zhǐ shi) (jí sih/ji² si⁶)
   "Pointing to matters", "indirect symbols" or "ideographs." The examples shown below were orginally formed by adding a dot above or below a horizontal line meaning up (above) or down (below).

   ˙— = 上   —˙ = 下

3. 形聲 (xíng shēng) (yìhing sìng/ying⁴ sing¹)
   "Determinative-phonetic characters." The combination of a radical suggesting the sense of the word plus a phonetic part indicating the pronunciation of the word. For example: river is written with the radical of three drops of water, indicating river is related to water, but it is pronounced as "hé" "hòh/hoh⁴" because the phonetic "kě" "hó/hoh²" is attached to it:

   氵   +   可   =   河
   water + (kě) hó/hoh² = (hé) hòh/hoh⁴ (river)

---

* Pronunciation guides are given in the order: (Pinyin) (Yale/Lau).

扌 + 足 = 捉

hand + (zú) jùk/juk¹ = (zhuō) jùk/juk¹ (catch)

4. 會意 (huì yì) (wuih yi/wui⁶ yi³)

"Meeting of ideas" or "associative compound." Two or more pictographs or ideographs are combined to form a new characters to indicate a new idea. For example: "good" is made up of a girl and a boy. It must be good to have both a daughter and a son in a family:

女 + 子 = 好   (daugter + son = good)
日 + 月 = 明   (sun + moon = bright)

Radicals

In common written Chinese, there are roughly 200 commonly used character fragments or *radicals* 部首 (bù shǒu) (boh sáu/bou⁶ sau²). Chinese characters are often composed of many fragments, and it is frequently possible to determine the approximate meaning of a character by examining the component pieces to determine the primary radical in the character.

For example, when the learners have learnt the radical for "mouth" (口), they will know that characters utilising this radical have some relationship with the mouth: 吃 is to eat, 唱 is to sing, and so on.

Armed with this knowledge, the learners will be able to infer the correct meaning of many of the Chinese characters they encounter, even if they are umfamiliar with the complete definition of the character. Here are some of the radicals:

人 = person   火 = fire   口 = mouth
手 = hand   女 = woman   木 = wood
目 = eye   子 = child   水 = water

Each Chinese character is pronounced as a single syllable and has its own meanings. Many ideas, thoughts and feelings are expressed by combining two or more simple characters to form a new character with a new meaning:

人   口   人口
people + mouth = population

iii

一	月	一月
one +	month =	January
火	山	火山
fire +	mountain =	volcano

There are altogether over 60,000 different Chinese characters and about 3,000 are commonly used. It sounds difficult to learn them all but it is not as difficult as it looks once you have mastered the rules and the structural framework.

Basic Strokes

Chinese characters are comprised of many strokes, each stroke has its own unique order in writing. This is called "pen order." One stroke is defined as the path from the point you put down your pen till you pick up your pen. For example, 刁 and 乙 is one stroke because you have to write it altogether without breaking it up. Examples of two-stroke characters are 人，刀 and those require three-stroke characters include 大，口，子. Some words are more complicated and contain more strokes such as 鸚 (parrot) has 28 strokes and 籲 (exhort) has 32.

There are eight basic strokes in Chinese writing:

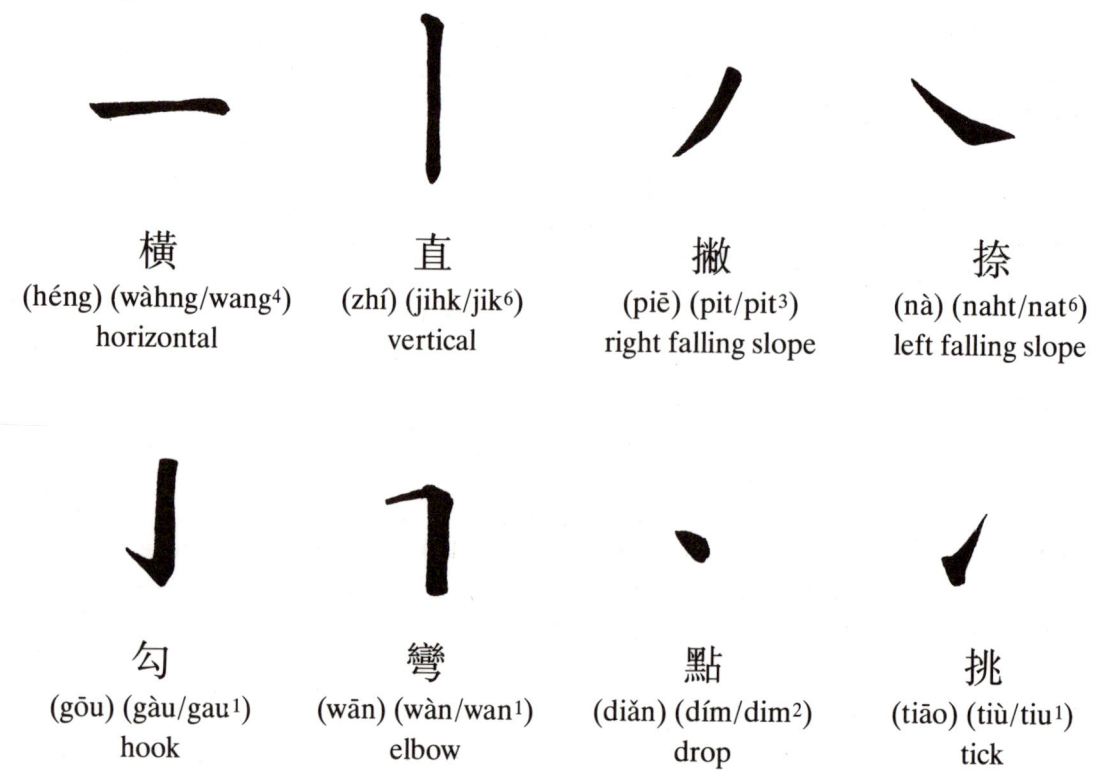

横
(héng) (wàhng/wang⁴)
horizontal

直
(zhí) (jihk/jik⁶)
vertical

撇
(piē) (pit/pit³)
right falling slope

捺
(nà) (naht/nat⁶)
left falling slope

勾
(gōu) (gàu/gau¹)
hook

彎
(wān) (wàn/wan¹)
elbow

點
(diǎn) (dím/dim²)
drop

挑
(tiāo) (tiù/tiu¹)
tick

The word 永 (yǒng) (wíhng/wing⁵), meaning "forever" has each of the above eight strokes in itself.

The order of the strokes is as follows:

The traditional way of handling a brush
to write Chinese characters.

The following table illustrates the variety of the shapes of a stroke and gives examples of how they appear in a character:

Stoke	Shape	Example
點 (drop)	、 ﹅ 丶 ˋ	小 衫 六 米 忙 池
橫 (horizontal)	一	十 木
直 (vertical)	丨	木
撇 (right falling slope)	丿 ノ ノ ノ	人 井 菜
捺 (left falling slope)	㇏ ㇏	大 是
挑 (tick)	㇀	拉 城
彎 (elbow)	㇈ ㇉ ㇌ ㄑ ㇋	日 山 紅 名 衣 朵 女 吸
勾 (hook)	亅 ㇁ ㄅ ㇆ ㇡ ㇟ ㇄	河 家 我 心 刀 他 汽 弟 孑

To help you understand the order of the stroke, here are some basic rules for you to follow:

Rule one: From top to bottom

   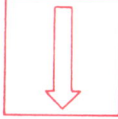 

Rule two: From left to right

     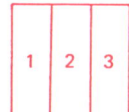

Rule three: First horizontal, then verticle

Rule four: First horizontal, then right falling slope

Rule five: First right falling slope, then left falling slope

Rule six: From outside to inside

   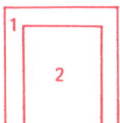

Rule seven: Go inside then close the door

   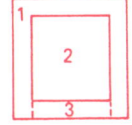

Rule eight: First middle, then preserve the symmetry

 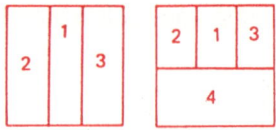

Apart from the above eight general rules, there are two more additional rules:

Rule nine: Three ways of writing dots

9a.   Write the dot first when it is on the left

斗 ➡ 丶 斗

9b.   Write the dot last when it is inside

寸 ➡ 十 寸

9c.   Write the dot last when it is on the top right

我 ➡ 我 我

Rule ten: First top right, then bottom left
            (usually for the radical 近 or 廷)

近 ➡ 斤 近

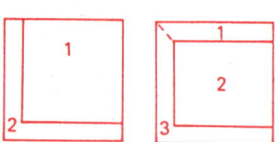

Chinese has many words which do not obey these rules. Pen order is not as simple as it seems! For these characters there is no choice but to remember their pen order by heart. For example, 水 (water) starts with the middle first and finishes with the strokes on the left and right. In contrast, the word 坐 (sit) is constructed by writing the left and right portions before the middle.

THE PUTONGHUA SOUNDS AND TONES

Putonghua is the official national language in China. It means "the common language." Pinyin was officially endorsed as the formal pronouciation system in China in 1958. The tone system of Putonghua is not as complicated as that of Cantonese.

There are four tones in Putonghua. The range of variation of pitch is represented by four degrees as shown in the following table:

Tone	high level	high rising	low dipping	high falling
Symbol				
Pitch level chart (5,4,3,2,1)	→	↗	∨	↘
Tone pitch	(5 → 5)	(3 → 5)	(2 → 1 → 4)	(5 → 1)
Example	媽	麻	馬	罵
Pinyin	mā	má	mǎ	mà
English meaning	mother	trouble	horse	scold

Four tones:
- ¯ keep the voice even
- ´ push the voice upward
- ˇ send the voice down then up
- ` push voice downward

Modern Putonghua has 430 sounds, far less than the number of characters. Therefore many characters share the same sound. The use of tone (pitch) is an important way to tell the difference in meaning of the same sound.

With characters having the same pronounciation but different tone, message might have completely different meanings depending on the tones used. For example:
- Mā ma mà mǎ. (Mother scolded the horse.)
- Mǎ mà mā ma. (The horse scolded mother.)
- Māma qí mǎ, mǎ màn, māma mà mǎ.
  (Mother rode a horse, the horse was slow, mother scolded the horse.)

Having the right tone is equally important as pronouncing the word correctly. Here are some tone practice for you to try:

yī 一 (one)	yí 姨 (aunt)	yǐ 椅 (chair)	yì 億 (hundred million)
wū 屋 (house)	wú 無 (none)	wǔ 五 (five)	wù 霧 (fog)
yān 烟 (cigarette)	yán 鹽 (salt)	yǎn 眼 (eye)	yàn 燕 (swallow)
mā 媽 (mother)	má 蔴 (hemp)	mǎ 馬 (horse)	mà 罵 (scold)
bā 八 (eight)	bá 拔 (pick)	bǎ 把 (hold)	bà 爸 (father)
shū 書 (book)	shú 熟 (ripe)	shǔ 鼠 (mouse)	shù 樹 (tree)

A word in Pinyin system has an intial and a final. Initials of f, l, m, n, s, y, w, b, d, g are roughly the same as in English. P, t, k are similar to English counterparts but are much more heavily aspirated. Here are the details:

Initial

b-	much as in bath	bā	爸
p-	as in pie	pá	爬
m-	as in man	mā	媽(妈)
f-	as in fun	fā	發(发)
d-	much as in dear	dā	大
t-	as in thick	tā	他
n-	as in nasty	nā	那
l-	as in large	lā	拉
z-	as in adds	zā	扎
c-	as in nuts	cā	擦
s-	as in sat	sā	殺(杀)

zh-	as in January	zhā	渣
ch-	as in challenge	chā	叉
sh-	as in shelter	shā	沙
r-	as in rent	rén	人
j-	as in genuine	jiā	家
q-	as in chew	qī	七
x-	as in siesta	xī	西
g-	much as in gun	gà	尬
k-	as in king	kā	卡
h-	as in loch	hā	哈

The vowels and final consonants

a	as in father	mā	媽 (妈)
o	as in saw	wǒ	我
e	much as in her	kě	可
i	as in yee	yī	一
er	as in "er indoors"	èr	二
u	much as in shoe	bù	不
ü	as in yew	lü	綠 (绿)
ai	as in aisle	tài	太
an	much as in bun	sàn	三
ang	as in bung (no hard 'g' sound)	shàng	上
ao	as in out	gāo	高
ei	as in day	mèi	妹
en	as in 'rock'n'roll	mén	門 (门)
eng	as in hunger ('u' flattened)	shēng	生
ia	as in yah	xià	下
ian	as in yen	tián	甜
iang	similar to young	liǎng	兩 (两)
iao	as in miaow	xiǎo	小
ie	as in yes	jiě	姐
in	as in sin	xīn	心
ing	much as in England	míng	名
iu	similar to eel	liù	六
ong	as in Jung	tóng	同
ou	as in soul	yǒu	有

ua	⎫	shuí	誰(谁)
uan	⎪	jué	絕(绝)
uen	⎬ no similar close	huā	花
ui	⎪ sounds as in English	yuán	圓(圆)
uan	⎪	guó	國(国)
uo	⎭		

The ü sound only appears after n-, l-, q-, x-, or on its own. The u sound appears after all inital consonants except j-, q-, x-, y-, so it is only after n- and l- that there can be any confusion between them.

Not all syllables are given a tone mark. This is because
1. grammatical particles do not have a tone, and so take their pitch from the words which come before them,
2. in two-syllable words, the second syllabe may be so little stressed as virtually not to have a tone, or
3. a few single-syllable words, shi (是 to be), lai (來 to come), and qu (去 to go), are commonly used without stressed tone in certain contexts. In such cases no tone mark is used.

As Chinese writing is pictograhic some characters are quite complicated. In 1956, the Chinese government began to simplify the structure of some characters to make them easier to write. These simplified characters have been widely and officially used ever since. A table showing the simplified form of the taught vocabulary in this book is shown in the "vocabulary list" at the end of the book.

THE CANTONESE SOUNDS AND TONES

Cantonese is a monosyllabic language that each word has only a single syllable. The various meanings of the each word are largely determined by the tone with which the word is pronounced.

Intonation is essential in reading Chinese because even if you produce the correct sound, associating it with a wrong tone can be a serious mistake: it will change the intended meaning. Good tones are life-time assets for Chinese language speakers.

A syllable in Cantonese has three elements:
1. an initial, the beginning consonant
2. a final, the ending of a syllable
3. a tone, the pitch level of the syllable

For example: You (你) is presented as:

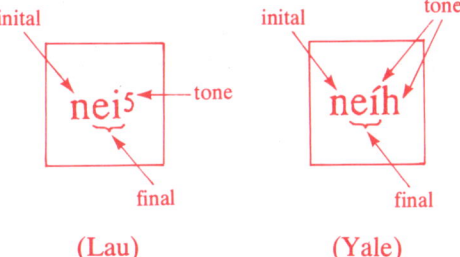

(Lau)　　　(Yale)

Cantonese has seven tones. Since most speakers do not distinguish between the high level and high falling tones, we commonly consider only 6 basic Cantonese tones as follows:

Tones	High Falling	Middle Rising	Middle Level	Low Falling	Low Rising	Low Level
Tone No.	1	2	3	4	5	6
Pitch Level Chart (5 4 3 2 1)	↘	↗	→	↘	↗	→
	(5 → 3)	(3 → 5)	(3 → 3)	(2 → 1)	(2 → 3)	(2 → 2)
Lau	foo¹	foo²	foo³	foo⁴	foo⁵	foo⁶
Yale	fù	fú	fu	fùh	fúh	fuh
Chinese	夫	苦	褲	符	婦	父
English meaning	husband	bitter	trousers	charm	woman	father

N.B. An * is used in the pronunciation systems to modify a tone in such a way that it is pronounced as in level 2.

xiii

There are 19 initials in Cantonese characters as illustrated in the following table:

Initial	Yale	Lau	Chinese	English
b	bà	ba1	爸	father
ch	chà	cha1	叉	fork
d	dà	da1	打	dozen
f	fà	fa1	花	flower
g	gà	ga1	家	home
gw	gwà	gwa1	瓜	melon
h	hà	ha1	蝦	shrimp
j	jì	ji1	知	to know
k	kà	ka1	卡	card
kw	kwà	kwa1	誇	to exaggerate
l	làai	laai1	拉	to pull
m	mà	ma1	媽	mother
n	neíh	nei5	你	you
ng	ńg	ng5	五	five
p	paak	paak3	泊	to park (a car)
s	sà	sa2	沙	sand
t	tà	ta1	他	he or she
w	wà	wa1	蛙	frog
y	yìn	yin1	煙	smoke

The Lau system has 53 Cantonese finals, which can be categorised into 9 groups:

1. **Group "a"**

Finals	as in
a	fast
ai	bite
au	pout
am	hum
an	sun
ang	rung
ap	sup
at	but
ak	duck

2. **Group "aa"**

Finals	as in
aai	island
aau	cow
aam	arm
aan	aunt
aang	aan + ng
aap	harp
aat	art
aak	ark

3. **Group "e"**

Finals	as in
e	merry
eng	length
ek	peck
ei	say
euh	her
eung	earn
euk	work

4. **Group "i"**

Finals	as in
i	bee
iu	ee + oo
im	seem
in	seen
ing	sing
ip	jeep
it	heat
ik	thick

5. **Group "o"**

Finals	as in
oh	saw
on	lawn
ot	bought
o	so
oi	toy
ong	long
ok	rock

6. **Group "oo"**

Finals	as in
oo	food
ooi	ruin
oon	noon
oot	foot

xv

7.   Group "u"

Finals	as in
ui	deuil*
un	nation
ut	put
ung	tongne
uk	took

8.   Group "ue"

Finals	as in
ue	she
uen	tune
uet	parachute

9.   Group Nasal

Finals	as in
m	mm
ng	singing

* No English equivalent, Pronouce in French.

1 TRIANGULAR RELATIONSHIPS

瑞士三角朱古力,點滴傳情意;甜蜜關係,微妙之至。

VOCABULARY

	Pinyin	Yale / Lau	English
情侶	qíng lǚ	chìhng léuih ching4 leui5	lovers
歡迎	huān yíng	fùn yìhng fun1 yìng4	welcome
關係	guānxi	gwàan haih gwaan1 hai6	relation/relationship
最	zuì	jeui jeui3	the most

SUPPLEMENTARY VOCABULARY

	Pinyin	Yale / Lau	English
三角形	sānjiǎo xíng	sàam gok yìhng saam1 gok3 ying4	triangle
圓形	yuán xíng	yùhn yìhng yuen4 ying4	circle/round
正方形	zhèng fāng xíng	jing fòng yìhng jing3 fong1 ying4	square
*朱古力	zhù gǔlì (qiǎo kè lì)	jyu gù lìk jue1 gwoo1 lik1	chocolate

USEFUL EXPRESSIONS

1. 受……歡迎

    e.g. 朱古力受人歡迎

    welcomed by… (popular with…)
    Pinyin: Zhù gǔli shou rén huān yíng
    Yale: Jyù gù lìk sauh yàhn fùn yìhng
    Lau: Jue1 gwoo1 lik1 sau6 yan4 fun1 ying4
    English: The chocolate (is) popular.
    (welcomed by people).

2. 最……

    e.g. 我最大，他最高。

    comparative adverb: showing the superlative degree
    Pinyin: Wǒ zuì dà, tā zuì gao.
    Yale: Ngóh jeui daaih, tà jeuì gòu.
    Lau: Ngoh5 jeui3 daai6, ta1 jeui3 gou1.
    English: I am the biggest, he is the tallest.

---

* 朱古力 in Cantonese = 巧克力(qiǎo kè lì) in Putonghua.

ADVERTISEMENT EXPLANATION

最受情侶歡迎的△(三角)關係。

Pinyin: Zuì shòu qíng lǚ huānyíng de (sān jiǎo) guān xi.
Yale: Jeui sauh chìhng léuih fùn yìhng dìk (sàam gok) gwàan haih.
Lau: Jeui3 sau6 chìng4 leui5 fun1 ying4 dik1 (saam1 gok3) gwaan1 hai6.
English: The most popular tranglar relationship with lovers.

ACTIVITY 1

Write the Chinese characters.

ACTIVITY 2

Match the pictures with suitable vocabulary.

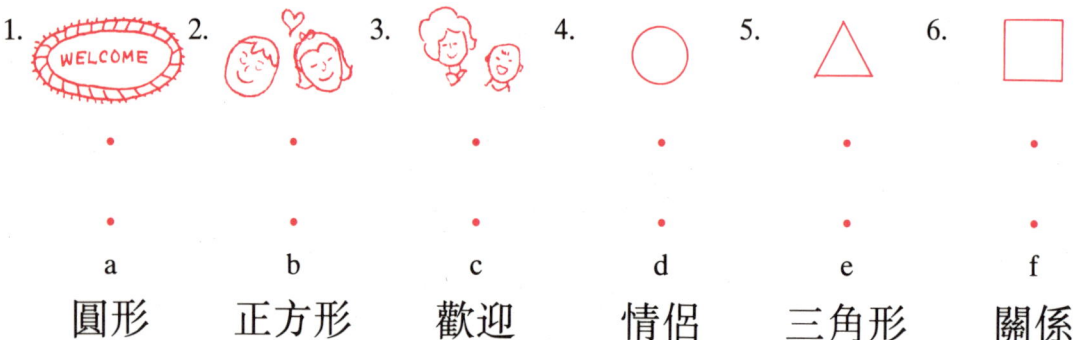

ACTIVITY 3

Study the following picture and fill in the blanks.

小 (small)　　大 (big)　　多 (many)

1. 圓形朱古力（　）大
2. （　）（　）形朱古力最小。
3. 正方形朱古力（　）多。

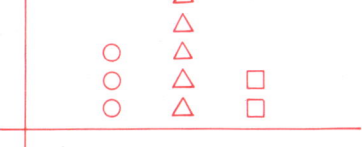

	P	Y	L	E
大	dà	daaih	daai6	big
小	xiǎo	síu	siu2	small
多	duō	dò	do1	many

ACTIVITY 4

True/False: Study the diagram and write <u>True</u> or <u>False</u> next to the sentences.

1. 正方形朱古力最受人歡迎。（　　　）
2. 三角形朱古力最多。（　　　）
3. 圓形朱古力最受人歡迎。（　　　）
4. 三角形朱古力最受人歡迎。（　　　）

ACTIVITY 5

Survey: Ask your friends what kind of shape of chocolate they like most. Draw a diagram to show your result and write your conclusion.

_____最受人歡迎。

2 DOUBLE HAPPINESS

VOCABULARY

	Pinyin	Yale / Lau	English
中式	zhōngshi	jùng sìk / jung¹ sik¹	Chinese style
結婚	jiéhūn	git fàn / git³ fan¹	wedding, marriage
*餅咭(卡)	bǐngkǎ	béng kàt / beng² kat¹	cake card
傳統	chuántǒng	chyùhn túng / chuen⁴ tung²	tradition, traditional
心	xīn	sàm / sam¹	heart
心意	xīnyi	sàm yi / sam¹ yi³	good thought
禮物	lǐ wù	láih maht / lai⁵ mat⁶	gift, present

SUPPLEMENTARY VOCABULARY

	Pinyin	Yale / Lau	English
一	yī	yàt / yat¹	one
**二(＝兩)	èr (liǎng)	yih (léuhng) / yi⁶ (leung⁵)	two
三	sān	sàam / saam¹	three
四	sì	sei / sei³	four
五	wǔ	ńgh / ng⁵	five
六	liù	luhk / luk⁶	six

---

* card 咭 ＝ 卡
** 兩(两) is more informal but used commonly both in speaking and writing.

七	qī	chàt chat¹	seven
八	bā	baat baat³	eight
九	jiǔ	gáu gau²	nine
十	shí	sahp sap⁶	ten

Popular beliefs about numbers

Lucky numbers

二, 2　sounds like easy (易)
三, 3　sounds like lively, energetic (生)
八, 8　sounds like prosperous and making money (發)
九, 9　sounds the same as long-lasting (久)

Unlucky numbers

四, 4　sounds like dying (死)
七, 7　a number related to Chinese funerals

MEASURE WORDS

一張餅咭	yī zhāng bǐngkǎ	yàt jèung béng kàt yat¹ jeung¹ beng² kat¹	a cake card
一份禮物	yī fèn lǐ wù	yàt fahn láih maht yat¹ fan⁶ lai⁵ mat⁶	a gift
一個蘋果	yī gè píngguǒ	yàt go pìhng gwó yat¹ goh³ ping⁴ gwo²	an apple
一個橙	yī gè chéng	yàt go cháang yat¹ goh³ chaang²	an orange
一杯茶	yī bèi chá	yàt bùi chàh yat¹ bui¹ cha⁴	a cup of tea
一個人	yī gè rén	yàt go yàhn yat¹ goh³ yan⁴	a person
一本書	yī běn shū	yàt bún sỳu yat¹ bun² sue¹	a book

Measure-words have three functions:
1. to show the quantitative unit of something: e.g. a cup of tea（一杯茶）; and to stress the nature and unit of a noun: e.g. a hand of cards（一手牌）.
2. as a collectvie noun as used in English.
3. to show a pictorial symbol, e.g. a head of a cow（一頭牛）, but they may also express one quality of their particular noun-group through a less obvious connection. So 張（张）'to stretch' is the measure for many flat-surfaced nouns (e.g. bed, table, picture, paper)（一張紙）and 個 signifies something round and compact: e.g. 一個橙.

Example:

a bed = a（張 of）bed　　　　　an apple = a（個 of）apple
a table = a（張 of）table　　　　an orange = a（個 of）orange
a paper = a（張 of）paper　　　a person = a（個 of）person
a card = a（張 of）card　　　　a book = a（本 of）book

USEFUL EXPRESSIONS

1.

	Pinyin	Yale / Lau	English
我	wǒ	ngóh / ngoh^5	I, me
你	nǐ	néih / nei^5	you
他	tā	tà / ta^1	he, him
她	tā	tà / ta^1	she, her
我們	wǒmen	ngóh mùhn / ngoh^5 moon^4	we, us
你們	nǐmen	néih mùhn / nei^5 moon^4	you
他們	tāmen	tāmen / tà mùhn / ta^1 moon^4	they, them

2. (somebody) 的 (noun) 。

e.g. 我的書。

…'s … (showing belonging)
Pinyin: Wǒ de shū.
Yale: Ngóh dīk sỳu.
Lau: Ngoh^5 dik^1 sue^1.
English: My book.

我的 你的 他的 她的	書	my your his her	book
我們的 你們的 他們的	書	our your their	book

ADVERTISEMENT EXPLANATION

囍   double happiness

This character is not found in the dictionary. It is actually a duplicated single character: 喜 meaning 'happiness.' This "double happiness" character is purely used for weddings, to give the partners an auspicious start to their new life.

一張中式結婚禮餅咭，一份傳統隆情的心意。

Pinyin: Yī zhāng zhōngshì jiéhūn lǐ bǐng kǎ, yī fèn chuántǒng lóngqíng de xīnyì.
Yale: Yàt jèung jùng sìk git fàn láih béng kat, yàt fahn chyùhn túng lùhng chìhng dìk sàm yi.
Lau: Yat[1] jeung[1] jung[1] sik[1] git[3] fan[1] lai[5] beng[2] kat[1], yat[1] fan[6] chuen[4] tung[2] lung[4] ching[4] dik[1] sam[1] yi[3].
English: A Chinese wedding cake card, (represents) a traditional nice thought full of deep feeling.

ACTIVITY 1

Write the Chinese characters.

糹 紝 結 女 婚 婚

結	婚									

| 食 | 飠 | 餅 | 口 | 吐 | 吐 | 咭 |

餅	咭									

| 一 | 亻 | 份 | 心 | 心 | 亠 | 音 | 意 |

一	份	心	意							

ACTIVITY 2

A magic square

Fill in the blank squares with a suitable number so that the same sum results when calculated horizontally, vertically and diagonally.

四	九		十五
十二	八		
十一		十	
		七	十一

ACTIVITY 3

Match the pictures with suitable phrases.

1. •   • a. 四個人

2. •   • b. 三份禮物

3. •   • c. 五個蘋果

4. •   • d. 九張餅咭

5. •   • e. 六杯茶

ACTIVITY 4

Draw pictures

1. 七個人　　　2. 八個橙　　　3. 十本書

ACTIVITY 5

Choose the most appropriate measure words to complete the phrases.

1. 三（個，隻，杯）茶。
2. 五（本，張，份）咭。
3. 二十（隻，份，張）禮物。
4. 十四（張，本，個）蘋果。
5. 九十（隻，份，個）人。

ACTIVITY 6

Starwars Game—Pair work

Instruction:
1. Draw 6 spaceships (3 short, 2 medium, 1 long, as shown below) on the game board without being seen by your partner. You can draw horizontally or vertically.
2. Take turns to shoot each other's spaceships by saying, for example,"三本書"，"五個橙"，"六個人"，etc.
3. If the named square has a spaceship, it will be destroyed. (A long spaceship needs 3 shoots to destroy it.)
4. You win the game when you have shot all your partner's spaceship.

Example:

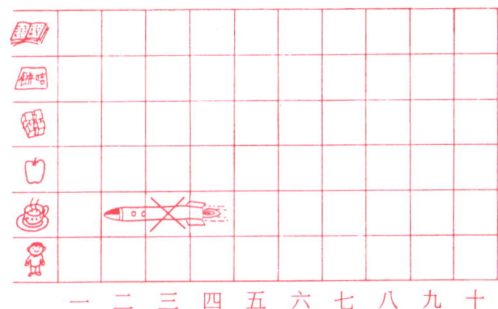

If you have drawn one of your spaceships as shown on the left and your partner has called out "三杯茶"(3 cups of tea) then your ship has got one shot. If your partner subsequently calls 四杯茶 and 兩杯茶, your whole ship will be destroyed. But if he calls out 一杯茶, you are safe because you have no ship in that square.

Now start the game:

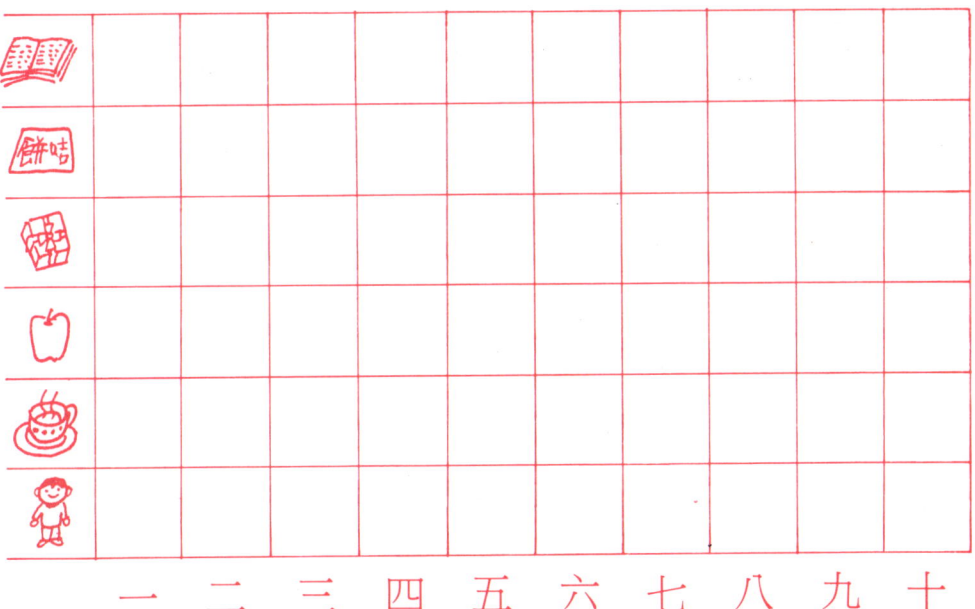

long spaceship: 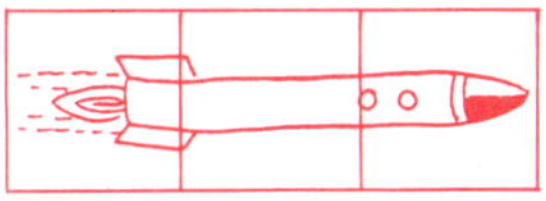 (takes up 3 squares)

medium spaceship: (takes up 2 squares)

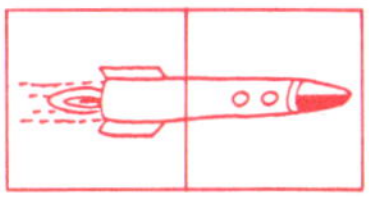

short spaceship: (takes up 1 square)

13

③ SOUR, SWEET, BITTER, HOT

超乎想像的甜酸苦辣，一一呈現在你的眼前。各具風味的傳統亞洲美食、特色甜點…由六個不同亞洲地區來港的名廚，在你面前烹調各式佳餚…無論午餐或晚餐，均有超過40款菜式供你選擇；款款都以地道材料精製而成，且不含味精，包括馳名遠近的醃製酸菜、酸瓜、辛辣海鮮及肉類等…寬敞舒適的環境，讓你更能盡情品嚐各款美饌…蒞臨奧麗太子酒店香味屋，猶如進入一個亞洲美食市集縮影，定能滿足你口腹之慾。為免苦候座位，請即致電訂座：377 6046

奧麗 太子酒店
九龍海港城

---

* Those words in shade are not proper words. They are made up words implying tastes can be mixed up.

14

VOCABULARY

		Pinyin	Yale Lau	English
酸		suān	sỳun suen¹	sour, sharp tast
甜		tián	tìhm tim⁴	sweet
苦		kǔ	fú foo²	bitter
辣		là	laaht laat⁶	chilli hot

SUPPLEMENTARY VOCABULARY

好吃		hǎo chī	hóu hek ho² hek³	delicious
吃		chī	hek hek³	eat
很		hěn	hán han²	very
這		zhè	jé je²	this

USEFUL EXPRESSIONS

1. 我的……(noun) 很……(adjective)，
   你的呢？

   e.g. 我的橙很甜，你的呢？

   My … (is) very …, and yours?
   Pinyin: Wǒ de chéng hěn tián, nǐ de ne?
   Yale: Ngóh dìk cháang hán tìhm, néih dìk nè?
   Lau: Ngo⁵ dik¹ chaang² han² tim⁴, nei⁵ dik¹ ne¹?
   English: My orange is very sweet, what about yours?

2. 這……(noun) 很……(adjective)。

   e.g. 這個橙很甜。

   This … (is) very …
   Pinyin: Zhè gè chéng hěn tián.
   Yale: Jé go cháang hán tìhm.
   Lau: Je² goh³ chaang² han² tim⁴.
   English: This orange (is) very sweet.

這	隻 本 杯 個	蘋果 書 茶 橙	很	好吃 大 苦 酸	。
This	(measure word)	apple book tea orange	(is) very	tasty. big. bitter. sour.	

ADVERTISEMENT EXPLANATION

酸 甜 苦 辣

Pinyin: Suān tián kǔ là
Yale: Sỳun tihm fú laaht
Lau: Suen[1] tim[4] foo[2] laat[6]
English: Sour, sweet, bitter, hot—these four tastes represent all the basic flavours of food. The expression also refers to life's experiences.

ACTIVITY 1

Write the Chinese characters.

丆 酉 酉' 酸

酸										

千 舌 甜 甜

甜										

艹 芏 苦

| 苦 | | | | | | | | | | |

立 辛 辢 辩 辣

| 辣 | | | | | | | | | | |

ACTIVITY 2

Match the pictures' tastes with the Chinese characters.

1. 酸 •   • a.

2. 甜 •   • b.

3. 苦 •   • c.

4. 辣 •   • d.

ACTIVITY 3

Rearrange the following characters to make sense of the sentence.

1. | 很 | 這 | 茶 | ☕ | 苦 | 。 |

   | | | | | | |

2. | 個 | 🍊 | 甜 | 很 | 這 | 。 |

   | | | | | | |

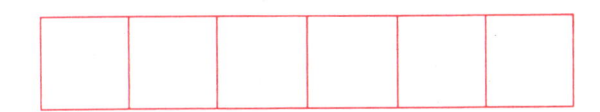

3. 很 個 🍎 好 這 吃 。

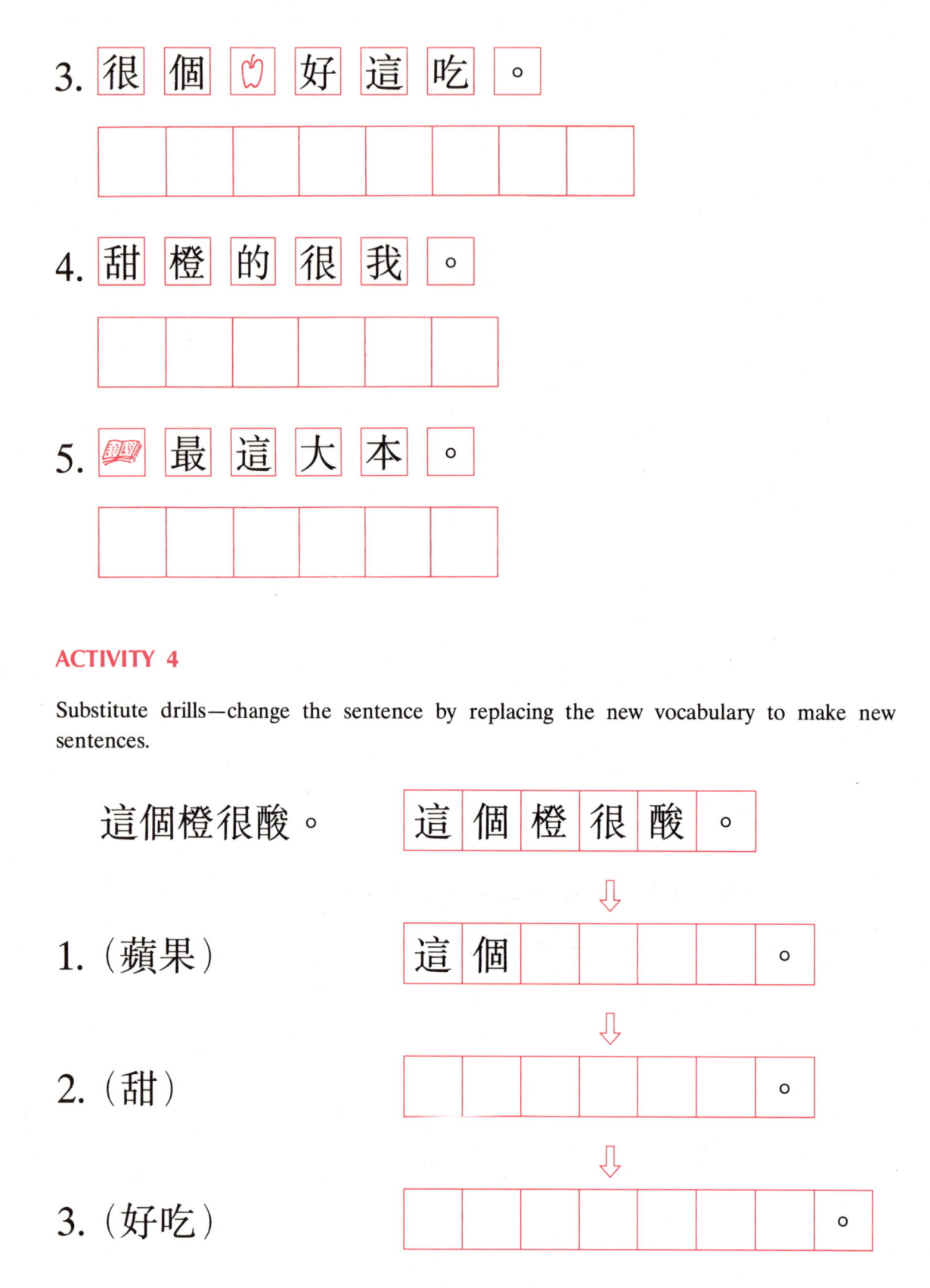

4. 甜 橙 的 很 我 。

5. 📖 最 這 大 本 。

ACTIVITY 4

Substitute drills—change the sentence by replacing the new vocabulary to make new sentences.

這個橙很酸。　　這 個 橙 很 酸 。

1.（蘋果）　　這 個 　 　 　 。

2.（甜）

3.（好吃）

4. （最）　⬇
　　|　|　|　|　|　|　|　|　|。

ACTIVITY 5

Bingo: 1. Choose and write the following words randomly in the square.
　　　　2. Listen to your teacher to say some vocabulary.
　　　　3. Circle the vocabulary if the word is spoken.
　　　　4. You win the game if you have circled 3 words in a row, column or diagonally.

甜　酸　苦　辣　蘋果　橙　書

好吃　受歡迎　情侶　圓形　三角形

4 MOTHER WANTS ME TO LEARN PIANO

媽媽想我學鋼琴

爸爸想我念哈佛

老師想我當律師

太太卻要我

MITSUBISHI PAJERO

往往你為了成全別人的期望，

放棄個人夢想。

但你心裡是否永遠願意只為

別人而活嗎？

自己的願望不一樣重要嗎？

讓你擁有自己的夢想吧！

我們特意獻上深受讚賞的

越野車PAJERO，讓你享受一份

真正的滿足感。

活出真我 滿足自己

留在家

但我選擇…

MITSUBISHI MOTORS
CREATING TOGETHER

VOCABULARY

	Pinyin	Yale / Lau	English
媽媽	māma	mà mà ma¹ ma¹	mother
爸爸	bà ba	bà bà ba¹ ba¹	father
老師	lǎo shī	lóuh sì lo⁵ si¹	teacher
太太	tài tai	taai táai taai³ taai²	wife
想	xiǎng	séung seung²	would like, wish
要	yào	yiu yiu³	want
學	xué	hohk hok⁶	learn
鋼琴	gāng qín	gong kàhm gong³ kam⁴	piano
哈佛	Hā fó	Hà faht Ha¹ fat⁶	Harvard (university)
律師	lǜ shī	leuht sì leut⁶ si¹	lawyer
留在家	liú zài jiā	làuh joih gà lau⁴ joi⁶ ga¹	stay home
但(＝但是)	dàn (dàn shì)	daahn (daahn sih) daan⁶ (daan⁶ si⁶)	but
選擇	xuǎnzé	sýun jaahk suen² jaak⁶	choose

SUPPLEMENTARY VOCABULARY

哥哥	gē ge	gò gò goh¹ goh¹	elder brother

弟弟	dì di	daih daih dai⁶ dai⁶	younger brother
姐姐	jiě jie	jé jé je² je²	elder sister
妹妹	mèi mei	muih muih mooi⁶ mooi⁶	younger sister

USEFUL EXPRESSIONS

1. ……，但……。

… but …

e.g. 這蘋果很大，但很酸。

Pinyin: Zhè píngguǒ hěn suān, dàn hěn tián.
Yale: Jé pìhng gwó hán daih, daahn hán sỳun.
Lau: Je² ping⁴ gwo² han² dai⁶, daan⁶ han² seun¹.
English: This apple (is) very big but (it is) very sour.

2. (subject) 想 (verb)。……想……。

… would like to (want to) …

e.g. 我想結婚。

Pinyin: Wǒ xiǎng jiéhūn.
Yale: Ngóh séung git fàn.
Lau: Ngo⁵ seung² git³ fan¹.
English: I want to get married.

3. (subject) 想 (someone) (verb)。……想……。

(subject) would like (someone) to (verb)

e.g. 媽媽想我結婚。

Pinyin: Māma xiǎng wo jiéhūn.
Yale: Mà mà séung ngóh git fàn.
Lau: Ma¹ ma¹ seung² ngo⁵ git³ fan¹.
English: (My) mother wants me to get married.

subject		someone	verb	
媽媽	想	我	結婚。	
爸爸		我	學	鋼琴。
太太		我	學	唱歌。
我		媽媽	留	在家。

Mother Father Wife I	want(s) (would like)	me me me mother	to get married. to learn to learn to stay	piano. singing. home.

ADVERTISEMENT EXPLANATION

媽媽想我學鋼琴，爸爸想我念哈佛，老師想我當律師，太太卻要我留在家，但我選擇……

Pinyin: Māma xiǎng wǒ xué gāngqín, bàba xiǎng wǒ niàn Hāfó, lǎoshī xiǎng wǒ dāng lǜshī, tàitai què yào wǒ liú zài jiā, dàn wǒ xuǎnzé…

Yale: Mà mà séung ngóh hohk gong kàlm, bà bà séung ngóh nihm Hà faht, lóuh sì séung ngóh dòng leuht sì, taai táai keuk yiu ngóh làuh joih gà, daahn ngóh sýun jaahk…

Lau: Ma[1] ma[1] seung[2] ngoh[5] hoh[6] gong[3] kam[4], ba[1] ba[1] seung[2] ngoh[5] nim[6] Ha[1] fat[6], lo[5] si[1] seung[2] ngoh[5] dong[1] leut[6] si[1], taai[3] taai[2] keuk[3] yiu[3] ngoh[5] lau[4] joi[6] ga[1], daan[6] ngoh[5] suen[2] jaak[6]…

English: (My) mother wants me to learn piano. (My) father wants me to study at Havard (university). (My) teacher wants me to be a lawyer. (My) wife, however, wants me to stay home. But I choose…

ACTIVITY 1

Write the Chinese characters.

女 妈 妈 媽

媽	媽								

丶 父 爸

爸	爸								

ナ 太
| 太 | 太 | | | | | | | | | | |

二 于 扏 我 我
| 我 | | | | | | | | | | | |

木 相 想
| 想 | | | | | | | | | | | |

亻 但 但
| 但 | | | | | | | | | | | |

ACTIVITY 2

Sentence pattern drill

鋼琴	piano
學鋼琴	learn piano
想學鋼琴	wants to learn piano
媽媽想學鋼琴	Mother wants to learn piano
媽媽想我學鋼琴	Mother wants me to learn piano
媽媽想我學鋼琴，但我想學唱歌	Mother wants me to learn piano, but I want to learn singing.

Now try to use the same pattern using 吃蘋果(eat an apple) and 吃橙(eat an orange) instead.
(i.e. Mother wants me to eat an apple, but I wants to eat an orange.)

Start:

| | 蘋 | 果 |

| 吃 | | |

| | | 蘋 | 果 |

| | | | 蘋 | 果 |

an apple
eat an apple
wants to eat an apple
Mother wants to eat an apple
Mother wants me to eat an apple
Mother wants me to eat an apple, but I want to eat an orange.

ACTIVITY 3

What would these people like to do? Walk through the maze to find out the answers. Fill in the conclusion when you finish.

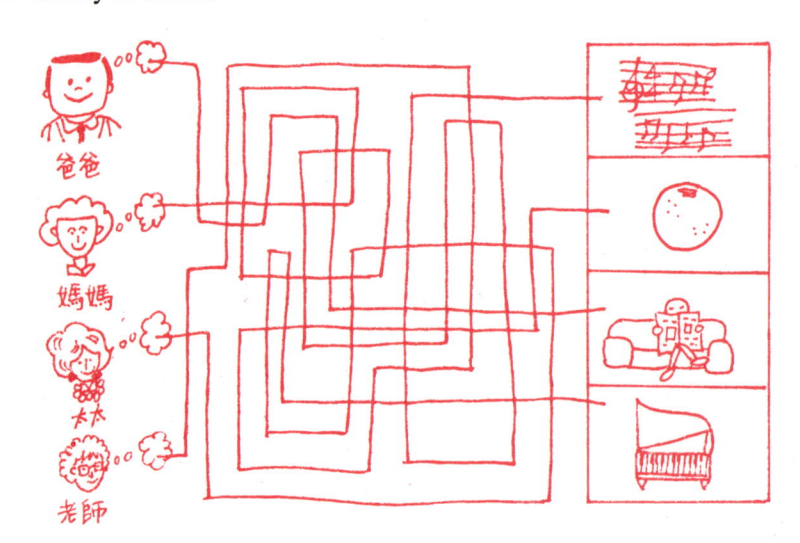

Results:
1. 爸爸想 •　　• a. 學唱歌。
2. 媽媽想 •　　• b. 學鋼琴。
3. 太太想 •　　• c. 留在家。
4. 老師想 •　　• d. 吃橙。

5 ARE YOU TOO THIN?

VOCABULARY

	Pinyin	Yale / Lau	English
你	nǐ	néih / nei[5]	You
是	shì	sih / si[6]	affirmative; verb to be: *is, am, are, was, were*
否	fǒu	fáu / fau[2]	negative; not to be: verb + not
太	tài	tai / tai[3]	too
瘦	shòu	sau / sau[3]	thin

SUPPLEMENTARY VOCABULARY

	Pinyin	Yale / Lau	English
是不是	shì bù shì	sih bàt sih / si[6] bat[1] si[6]	yes or no
肥(肥胖)	féi (féi pàng)	fèih (fèih buhn) / fei[4] (fei[4] boon[6])	fat
高	gào	gòu / go[1]	tall, high
矮	ǎi	ái / ai[2]	short
輕	qīng	hèng / heng[1]	light
重	zhòng	chúhng / chung[5]	heavy
有	yǒu	yáuh / yau[5]	have, has

USEFUL EXPRESSIONS

1. (subject)……是(noun)……。

   Affirmative statement:
   (subject)………… is, am, are, was, were (noun)………

e.g. 我是 Peter。   I am Peter.

我 你 他	是	Peter。

I You He	am are is	Peter.

2. ……(subject)不是(noun)……。

Negative statement:
(subject) verb to be + not (noun)

e.g. 我不是 Peter。   I am not Peter.

我 你 他	不是	Peter。

I You He	am not are not is not	Peter.

3. ……是不是……？

Question forms: Are you……?
Is she/he……?

e.g. 你是不是太肥胖？

Pinyin: Nǐ shì bù shì tài féi pàng?
Yale: Néih sih bàt sih tai fèih buhn?
Lau: Nei5 si6 bat1 si6 tai3 fei4 boon6?
English: Are you too fat?

note: 是否(only in written form) = 是不是(both in written and spoken form)

subject	verb + neg. verb	too	adjective	
你 她 他 我 它	是不是	太	瘦 高 矮 肥 大	？

* direct translation

You She He I It	are or are not is or is not is or is not am or am not is or is not	too	thin? tall? short? fat? big?

English pattern

Are you too thin? Is she too tall? Is he too short? Am I too fat? Is it too big?

Responses:

是。	shì	sih si⁶	Yes
不是。	bùshì	bàt sih bat¹ si⁶	No

4. (subject)不是(adjective)。   … not … (showing negative form)

e.g. 我不是肥胖。

= 我不肥胖。

Pinyin: Wǒ bù shì féi pàng.
Yale: Ngóh bàt sih fèit buhn.
Lau: Ngo⁵ bat¹ si⁶ feit⁴ boon⁶.
English: I am not fat.

ADVERTISEMENT EXPLANATION

你是否太瘦？

Pinyin: Nǐ shì fǒu tài shòu?
Yale: Néih sih fáu tai sau?
Lau: Nei⁵ si⁶ fau² tai³ sau³?
English: Are you too thin?

ACTIVITY 1

Write the Chinese characters.

亻 你 你

你											

旦 旱 是

是											

广 疒 疒 疒 瘦

| 瘦 | | | | | | | | | | | |

ACTIVITY 2

Four people, 甲，乙，丙，丁 have been given four different presents for their party. Describe who got what according to their body builds.

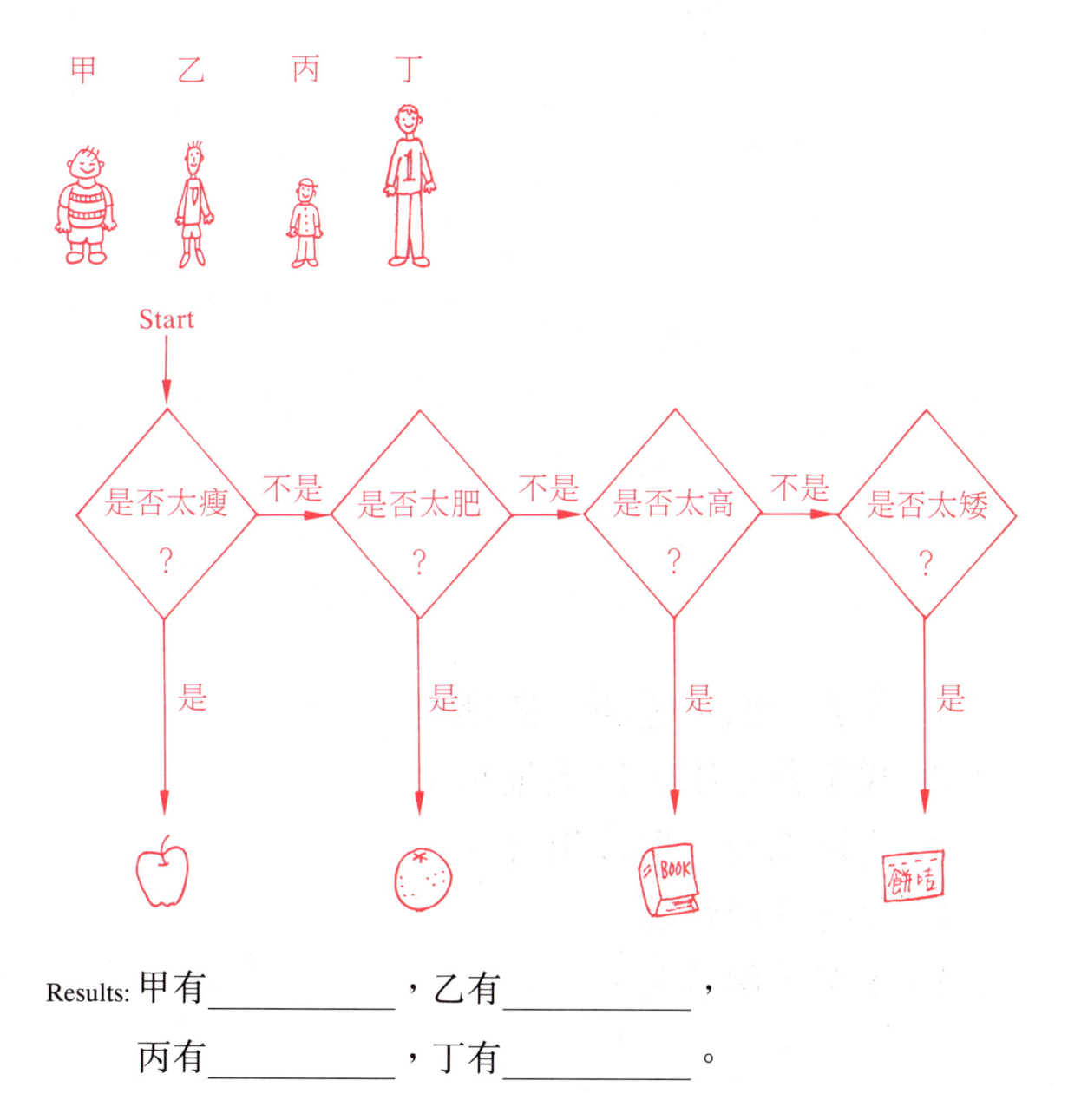

甲　乙　丙　丁

Start

是否太瘦？ →不是→ 是否太肥？ →不是→ 是否太高？ →不是→ 是否太矮？

↓是　　　　　↓是　　　　　↓是　　　　　↓是

(apple)　　　(orange)　　　(book)　　　(餅干)

Results: 甲有_____，乙有_____，
丙有_____，丁有_____。

ACTIVITY 3

This is a family picture of Peter's. He is describing his family. Which sentences are true? Write T for the true sentences and F for those which are false.

☐ 1. 我有一個爸爸和一個媽媽。

☐ 2. 我爸爸不肥，但他很高。

☐ 3. 我媽媽瘦，但她很矮。

☐ 4. 我有三個妹妹。

☐ 5. 我有一個弟弟。

ACTIVITY 4

Refer to the same picture of Peter's.
Give true answers to the following questions about Peter's family by saying "是" or "不是".

1. Peter 的爸爸是不是肥胖？　　　　　_____

2. Peter 的媽媽是不是瘦？　　　　　　_____

3. Peter 的妹妹是不是高？　　　　　　_____

4. Peter 的弟弟是不是矮？　　　　　　_____

ACTIVITY 5

Here are 3 family pictures that belong to Mary, Susan and Amy. Which ones correspond to the statements given below?

☐ Amy: 我有兩個弟弟。

☐ Susan: 我有一個妹妹。

☐ Mary: 我有一個哥哥。

6 THE HEAD

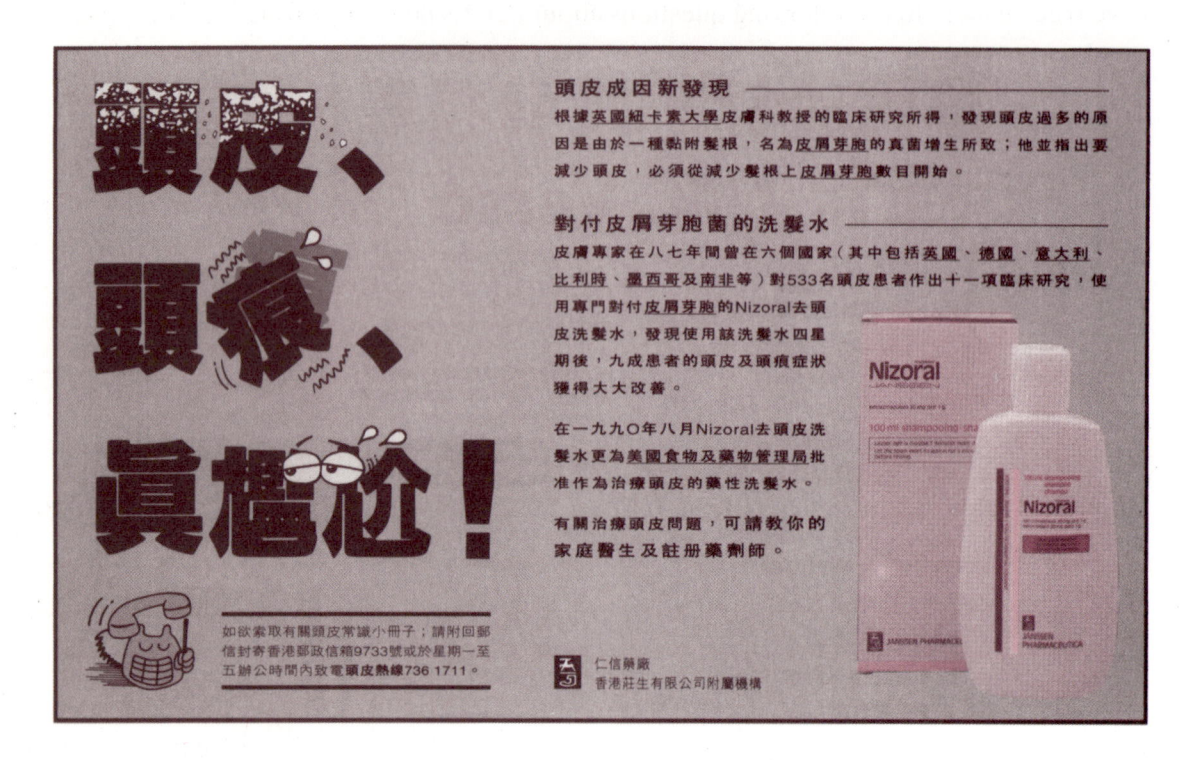

VOCABULARY

	Pinyin	Yale / Lau	English
頭	tóu	tàuh / tau⁴	head
皮	pí	pèih / pei⁴	skin
頭皮	tóupí	tàuh pèih / tau⁴ pei⁴	dandruff
痕	hěn	hàhn / han⁴	itchy
真	zhēn	jàn / jan¹	real, really
尷尬	gānggà	gaam gaai / gaam³ gaai³	embarrasing

SUPPLEMENTARY VOCABULARY

眼	yǎn	ngáahn ngaan5	eye(s)
耳	ěr	yíh yi5	ear(s)
口 (＝嘴)	kǒu (zuǐ)	háu (jéui) hau2 (jeui2)	mouth
鼻 (＝鼻子)	bízi	beih (beih jí) bei6 (bei6 ji2)	nose
面	miàn	minh min6	face
痛	tòng	tung tung3	ache, pain
頭髮	tóufà	tàuh faat tau4 faat3	hair
長	cháng	chèuhng cheung4	long
短	duǎn	dýun duen2	short

MEASURE WORDS

一個口	yī gè kǒu	yàt go háu yat1 goh3 hau2	a mouth
一隻耳	yī zhī ěr	yàt jek yíh yat1 jek3 yi5	an ear
一隻眼	yī zhī yǎn	yàt jek ngáahn yat1 jek3 ngaan5	an eye
*一條頭髮	yī tiáo tóufà	yàt tìuh tàuh faat yat1 tiu4 tau4 faat3	a hair

---

* The measure word 條 is used for something long and thin.
一根頭髮 (根 gēn, gàan, gaan1), a (root of) hair is also commonly used in Putonghua and in book publication.

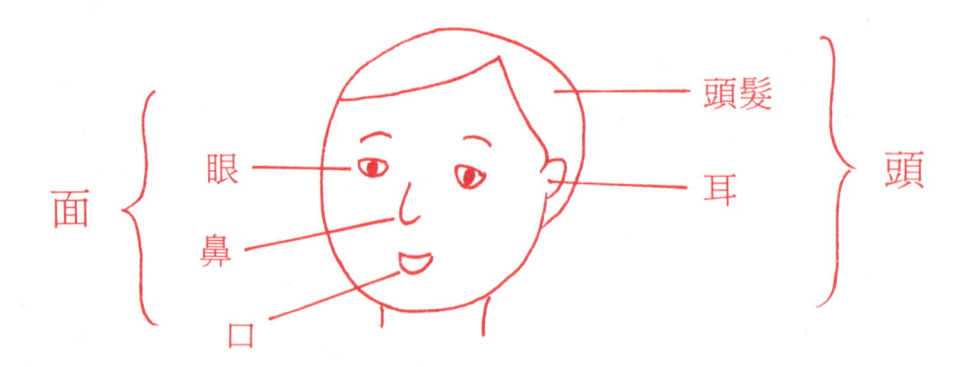

[Diagram of a head labeling: 頭髮 (hair), 耳 (ear), 眼 (eye), 鼻 (nose), 口 (mouth), 面 (face), 頭 (head)]

USEFUL EXPRESSIONS

這⸺(noun)⸺真⸺(adj)⸺。

e.g. 這個蘋果真好吃！

This ⸺(noun)⸺ (is) really ⸺(adj)⸺

Pinyin: Zhègè píngguǒ zhēn hǎo chī!
Yale: Jé go pìhng gwó jàn hóu hek!
Lau: Je² goh³ ping⁴ gwo² jan¹ hoh² hek³!
English: This apple (is) really tasty!

這	鋼琴 橙 本書	真	受人歡迎 酸 大	！

This	piano orange book	(is) really	popular! sour! big!

ADVERTISEMENT EXPLANATION

頭皮、頭痕、真尷尬！

Pinyin: Tóupí, tóuhěn, zhēn gāngà.
Yale: Tàuh pèih, tàuh hàhn, jàn gaam gaai.
Lau: Tau⁴ pei⁴, tau⁴ han⁴, jan¹ gaam³ gaai³.
English: Dandruff, itchy head, (It is) really embarrassing!

ACTIVITY 1

Write the Chinese characters.

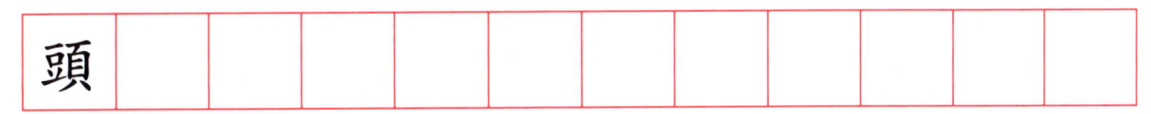

豆 豇 頭 頭

| 頭 | | | | | | | | | | | |

厂 户 皮

| 皮 | | | | | | | | | | | |

疒 疕 痕

| 痕 | | | | | | | | | | | |

十 市 直 直 真

| 真 | | | | | | | | | | | |

ACTIVITY 2

Match the pictures with suitable vocabulary.

1. • • a. 眼

2. • • b. 耳

3. • • c. 頭髮

4. • • d. 口

5. • • e. 鼻

ACTIVITY 3

What would you say when you see these situations?

1. 她的頭髮 □ □ ！

2. 他的爸爸 □ □ ！

3. 這蘋果 □ □ □ ！

ACTIVITY 4

Your friend was abducted by aliens. Now he has been brought back to earth. Here is his description of an alien. Draw the picture according to his report.

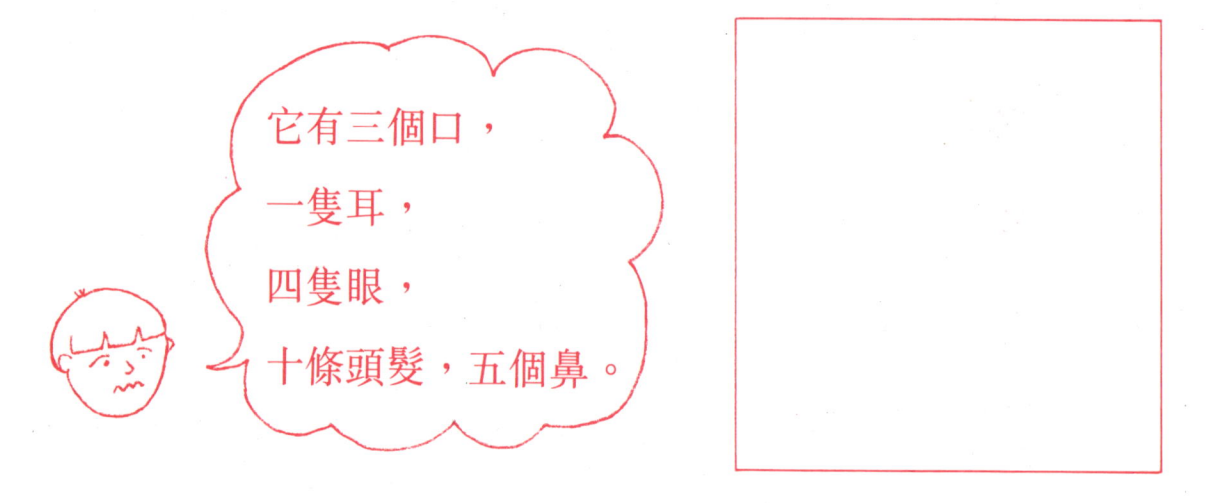

它有三個口，
一隻耳，
四隻眼，
十條頭髮，五個鼻。

7 CATCH THE MINUTES AND SECONDS

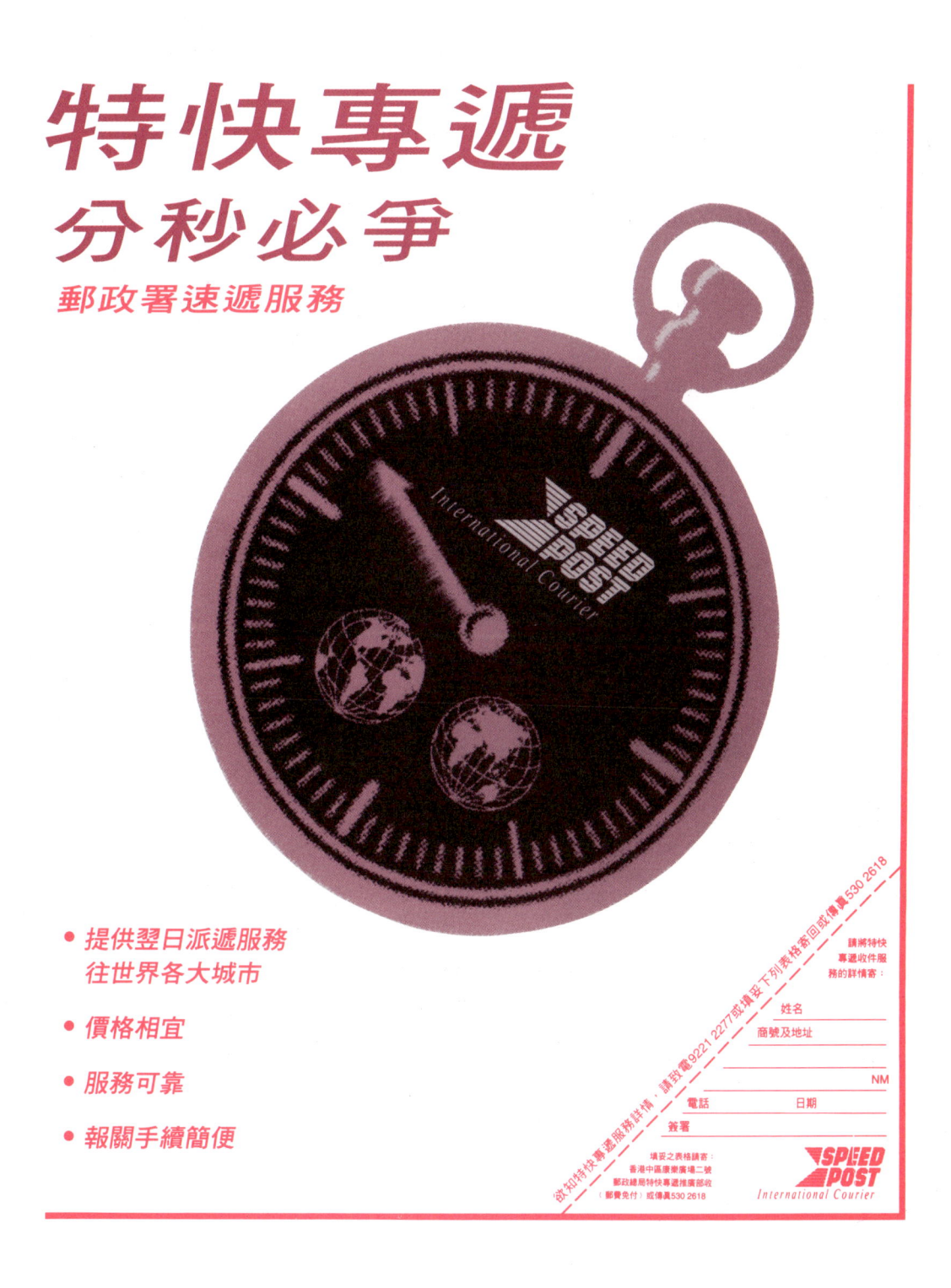

特快專遞
分秒必爭
郵政署速遞服務

- 提供翌日派遞服務往世界各大城市
- 價格相宜
- 服務可靠
- 報關手續簡便

欲知特快專遞服務詳情，請政電9221 2277或填妥下列表格寄回或傳真530 2618

請將特快專遞收件服務的詳情寄：

姓名 _____
商號及地址 _____
_____ NM
電話 _____ 日期 _____
簽署 _____

填妥之表格請寄：
香港中區康樂廣場二號
郵政總局特快專遞推廣部收
（郵費免付）或傳真530 2618

SPEED POST
International Courier

VOCABULARY

	Pinyin	Yale Lau	English
快	kuài	faai faai3	quick, fast
特別	tèbié	dahk biht dak6 bit6	special, super
專遞	zhuándì	jyùn daih juen1 dai6	special delivery
分	fēn	fàn fan1	minute
秒	miǎo	míuh miu5	second
必	bì	bìt bit1	must, should
爭	zhēng	jàng jang1	contend, fight

SUPPLEMENTARY VOCABULARY

時	shì	sìh si4	hour
時間	shíjiàn	sìh gaan si4 gaan3	time
現在	xiànzài	yihn joih yin6 joi6	now
慢	màn	maahn maan6	slow
什麼	shenmó	sahm mò sam6 moh1	what

USEFUL EXPRESSIONS

1. 現在是什麼時間？

   Pinyin: Xiànzài shì shenmó shíjiàn?
   Yale: Yihn joih sih sahm mò sìh gaan?
   Lau: Yin6 joi6 si6 sam6 moh1 si4 gaan3?
   English: Now is what time?
   (= What is the time now?)

2. 現在是……時……分。 Now (it) is … hour … minute.

   e.g. 現在是三時十分

   Pinyin: Xiànzài shì sān shí shí fēn.
   Yale: Yihn joih sih sàam sìh sahp fàn.
   Lau: Yin6 joi6 si6 saam1 si4 sap6 fan1.
   English: Now (it) is three (hour) ten (minute).

ADVERTISEMENT EXPLANATION

分 秒 必 爭

"Catch the minute and second" implies "rush, haste." It is an useful expression for busy people's life. It is similar to the English expression "time waits for no man."

特快專遞，分秒必爭。

Pinyin: Tè kuài zhuān dì, fēn miǎo bì zhēng.
Yale: Dahk fáai jỳun daih, fàn míuh bìt jàng.
Lau: Dak6 faai3 juen1 dai6, fun1 miu5 bit1 jang1.
English: Super quick special delivery, fight for every minute and second.

ACTIVITY 1

Write the Chinese characters.

忄 忄 快

快											

日 旷 時

時											

八 分

| 分 | | | | | | | | | | | |

千 利 秒 秒

| 秒 | | | | | | | | | | | |

ACTIVITY 2

Study the following Chinese expressions describing time, then draw the hands of the clock accordingly.

e.g.

七時正
P: qī shí zhèng
Y: chàt sìh jīng
L: chat¹ si⁴ jing³

七時一刻
P: qī shí yī kè
Y: chàt sìh yàt hàk
L: chat¹ si⁴ yat¹ hak¹

七時半
P: qī shí bàn
Y: chàt sìh bun
L: chat¹ si⁴ boon³

七時五十分
P: qī shí wǔ shí fēn
Y: chàt sìh ńgh sahp fàn
L: chat¹ si⁴ ng⁵ sap⁶ fan¹

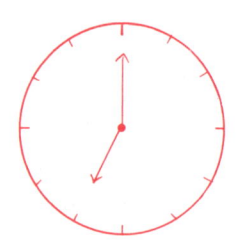

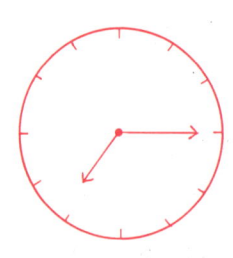

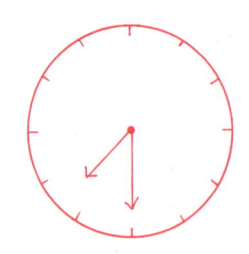

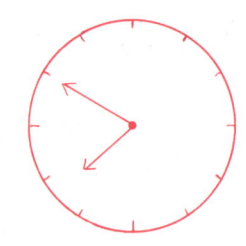

1. 九時半

2. 六時正

3. 四時三刻

4. 八時三十五分

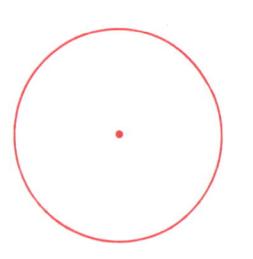

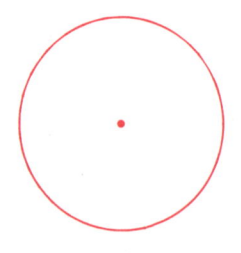

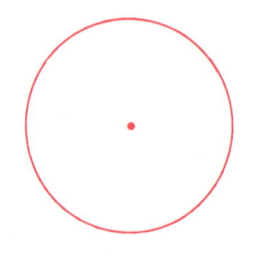

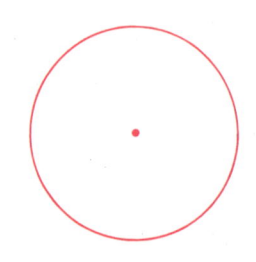

ACTIVITY 3

This is Mary's schedule for Monday.

1. Mary 什麼時間吃蘋果？
   _____

2. 她什麼時間吃朱古力？
   _____

3. 她吃不吃餅？
   _____

4. 她什麼時間學鋼琴？
   _____

ACTIVITY 4

Match the opposites.

1. 快 •　　　　• a. 矮
2. 肥 •　　　　• b. 短
3. 甜 •　　　　• c. 苦
4. 高 •　　　　• d. 瘦
5. 長 •　　　　• e. 慢
6. 大 •　　　　• f. 小

⑧ MID-AUTUMN FESTIVAL

VOCABULARY

		Pinyin	Yale / Lau	English
中		zhōng	jùng / jung¹	middle, mid-
秋		qiū	chàu / chau¹	autumn
心意		xīnyì	sàam yi / saam¹ yi³	nice thought
傳		chuán	chyùhn / chuen⁴	to pass, send
人		rén	yàhn / yan⁴	people
月		yuè	yuht / yuet⁶	moon
兩		liǎng	léuhng / leung⁵	two
團圓		tuányuán	tyùhn yùhn / tuen⁴ yuen⁴	united
圓		yuán	yùhn / yuen⁴	round
月餅		yuèbǐng	yuht béng / yuet⁶ beng²	moon cake

SUPPLEMENTARY VOCABULARY

中秋節		zhōngqiūjié	jùng chàu jit / jung¹ chau¹ jit³	mid-autumn festival
春		chūn	chèun / cheun¹	spring
夏		xià	hah / ha⁶	summer
冬		dōng	dùng / dung¹	winter

ADVERTISEMENT EXPLANATION

中秋心意傳，人月兩團圓。

Pinyin: Zhōng qiū xīnyì chuán, rén yuè liǎng tuányuán.
Yale: Jùng chàu sàam yi chyuhn, yàhn yuht léuhng tyùhn yùhn.
Lau: Jung¹ chau¹ saam¹ yi³ chuen⁴, yan⁴ yuet⁶ leung⁵ tuen⁴ yuen⁴.
English: People get together to be united just as the moon is round, full and perfect.
* Direct translation:
  (In) mid-autumn festival, (we) pass good thought (to people), both people and the moon are united together.

中秋節　Mid-autumn Festival

Mid-autumn festival is one of the most popular Chinese festivals. The story behind it is set thousands of years ago. There were nine suns in the sky and all the people were suffering from the extreme heat. A brave man named 后羿 (hòu yì, hauh ngaih, hau⁶ ngai⁶) shot down eight of the suns and the only sun left gave people just the right amount of warmth. In gratitude, the people made him King.

Years later the king had become greedy and wanted to live forever. He asked his doctors to make him a special pill that would give him eternal life.

His queen 嫦娥 (cháng é, sèuhn ngòh, suen⁴ ngo⁴) knew that he was no longer a good king and it would only do harm to the people if he should live forever, so she took the pill and swallowed it when it was just ready to be presented to the king. The king was very angry and tried to punish her but the queen slowly flew towards the moon and stayed there forever. Nowadays, we can see 嫦娥 quite clearly on the face of the moon during the mid-autumn festival.

The "Moon Cake" Legend

Moon cakes originated in the Yuan Dynasty and were used to hide secret messages about a planned rebellion against the mongols.

The people involved in the revolution needed a way of telling prisoners held in jail when the revolution would begin and thus when they would be freed: when the moon next became full.

The solution to the problem was to bake cakes with messages hidden inside them. The cakes could be given to the prisoners without their guards becoming suspicious—food is very important to the Chinese and not even the most evil guard would question a prisoner's desire for good food!

When the prisoners received the cakes they knew when they should revolt against their guards and break out of the prison.

The revolution was successful and to this day, people celebrate the deposition of an evil and unpopular emperor.

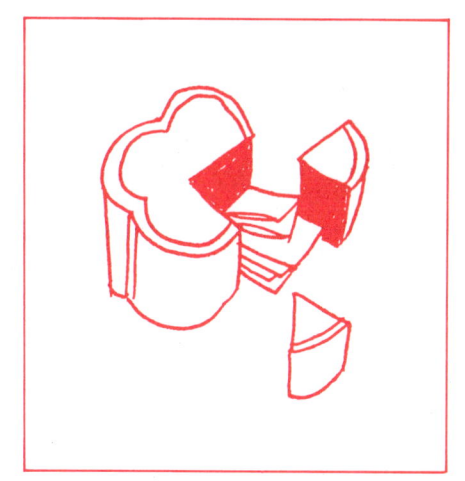

ACTIVITY 1

Write the Chinese characters.

口 中

中											

千 禾 秒 秋

秋											

人

人											

丿 月

月									

一 厂 币 两

两									

ACTIVITY 2

Match the seasons with the suitable pictures.

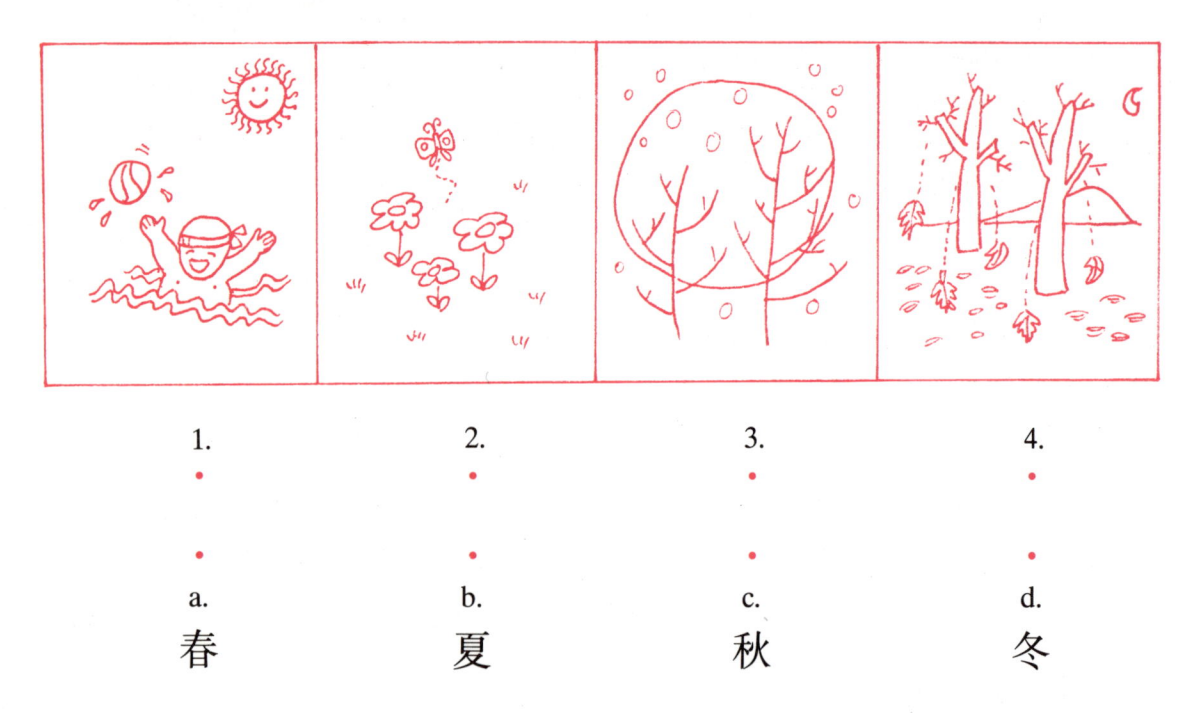

1.   2.   3.   4.

a.   b.   c.   d.
春   夏   秋   冬

ACTIVITY 3

Domino game

This game can be played by one to four people.
To play the game, you have to cut the card that are enclosed at the end of book (entitled "Unit 8"). The cards can be made into 20 dominos.
Each domino has two faces: a picture face and a character face.

48

Instructions for play:

1. The dealer should shuffle the cards.
2. The dealer should distribute the cards equally to each player.
3. The dealer should lay down one of his cards.
4. The players should take turns to match the cards in their "hand" with the cards placed out by other players: a picture should be placed next to a matching word and vice-versa. A person can 'pass' if he or she does not have a card matching the word or picture that is at the end of the line of cards already laid out.
5. The winner is the person who is the first to lay down all of his or her cards.

9 MERRY CHRISTMAS

聖誕快樂！新年進步！

VOCABULARY

	Pinyin	Yale / Lau	English
*聖誕	shèng dàn	sing dan sing³ dan³	Christmas
快樂	kuài lè	fai lohk fai³ lok⁶	happy
新	xīn	sàan saan¹	new

---

* The formal way to write Christmas is 聖誕.
  But it is generally acceptable to write Christmas in a colloquial way as 聖誕 nowadays.

新年	xīn nián	sàan nìhn saan¹ nin⁴	new year
進步	jìn bù	jeun bouh jeun³ bo⁶	progress (prosperous) improve, get better

SUPPLEMENTARY VOCABULARY

生日	shēng rì	sàng yaht sang¹ yat⁶	birthday
身體	shēn tǐ	sàn tái san¹ tai²	body
健康	jiàn kāng	gihn hòng gin⁶ hong¹	healthy
祝	zhù	jùk juk¹	wish
學業	xué yè	hohk yihp hok⁶ yip⁶	study performance
並賀	bìng hè	bihng hoh bing⁶ hoh⁶	and celebrate
幸福	xìng fú	hahng fùk hang⁶ fook¹	lucky

USEFUL EXPRESSIONS

祝你……。

e.g. 祝你生日快樂。

Wish you…

Pinyin: Zhù nǐ shēngrì kuàilè.
Yale: Jùk néih sàng yaht fai lohk.
Lau: Juk¹ nei⁵ sang¹ yat⁶ fai³ lok⁶.
English: Wishing you birthday happy.

祝你	生日 新年 聖誕	快樂。

Wishing you	birthday New Year Christmas	happy.

ADVERTISEMENT EXPLANATION

聖誕快樂！新年進步！

Pinyin: Shèng dàn kuài lè, xīn nián jìn bù
Yale: Sing dan fai lohk, sàan nìhn jeun bouh
Lau: Sing3 dan3 fai3 lok6, saan1 nin4 jeun3 bo6
English: Christmas happy! New year prosperous!

Note: As can be imagined, these expressions are widely used. At Christmas and New Year, you will see these phrases everywhere: festooned upon the sides of hotels and office blocks, in newspapers and advertisements and on cards. You may even see them on the sides of the 'star' ferries, buses, taxis and trams.

ACTIVITY 1

Write the Chinese characters.

聖誕

快樂

新年

進步

ACTIVITY 2

Match the Chinese blessings with suitable English expressions.

1. 新年快樂！ •   • a. Good health!

2. 聖誕快樂！ •   • b. Study performance getting better!

3. 生日快樂！ •   • c. Happy New Year!

4. 身體健康！ •   • d. Merry Christmas!

5. 學業進步！ •   • e. Happy Birthday!

ACTIVITY 3

What are these people saying? Write the suitable Chinese expression in the bubbles.

1   2   3

ACTIVITY 4

Sing this song "生日快樂". The tune is the same as in the song "Happy Birthday to you" in English.

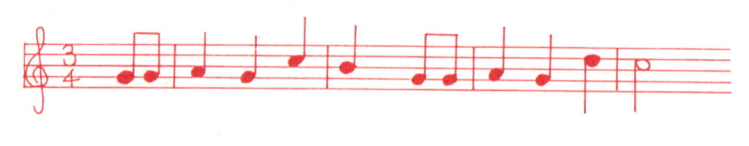

祝你生日快樂(2)

Pinyin: Zhù nǐ shēngrì kuài lè. (2)
Yale: Jùk néih sàng yaht fai lohk. (2)
Lau: Juk¹ nei⁵ sang¹ yat⁶ fai³ lok⁶ (2)
English: Happy birthday to you (2)

祝你生日快樂,祝你生日快樂。

Pinyin: Zhù nǐ shēngrì kuài lè, zhù nǐ shēngrì kuài lè.
Yale: Jùk néih sàng yaht fai lohk, jùk néih sàng yaht fai lohk.
Lau: Juk¹ nei⁵ sang¹ yat⁶ fai³ lok⁶, juk¹ nei⁵ sang¹ yat⁶ fai³ lok⁶.
English: Happy birthday to you, happy birthday to you.

Sing this song "聖誕快樂". The tune is the same as in the song "We wish you a merry Christmas".

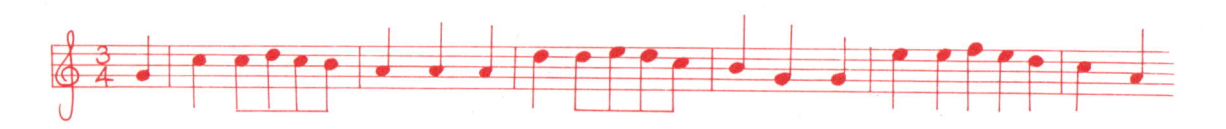

我們祝你們聖誕快樂,(3)

Pinyin: Wǒ men zhù nǐ men shèng dàn kuài lè, (3)
Yale: Ngóh mùhn jùk néih mùhn sing dan fai lohk, (3)
Lau: Ngoh⁵ moon⁴ juk¹ nei⁵ moon⁴ sing³ dan³ fai³ lok⁶, (3)
English: We wish you a merry Christmas, (3)

並賀新年幸福。

Pinyin: bìng hè xīn nián xìng fú.
Yale: bihng hoh sàan nìhn hahng fùk.
Lau: bing[6] hoh[6] saan[1] nin[4] hang[6] fook[1].
English: and a happy new year.

ACTIVITY 5

Design the following cards and write the inside blessings for your friends.

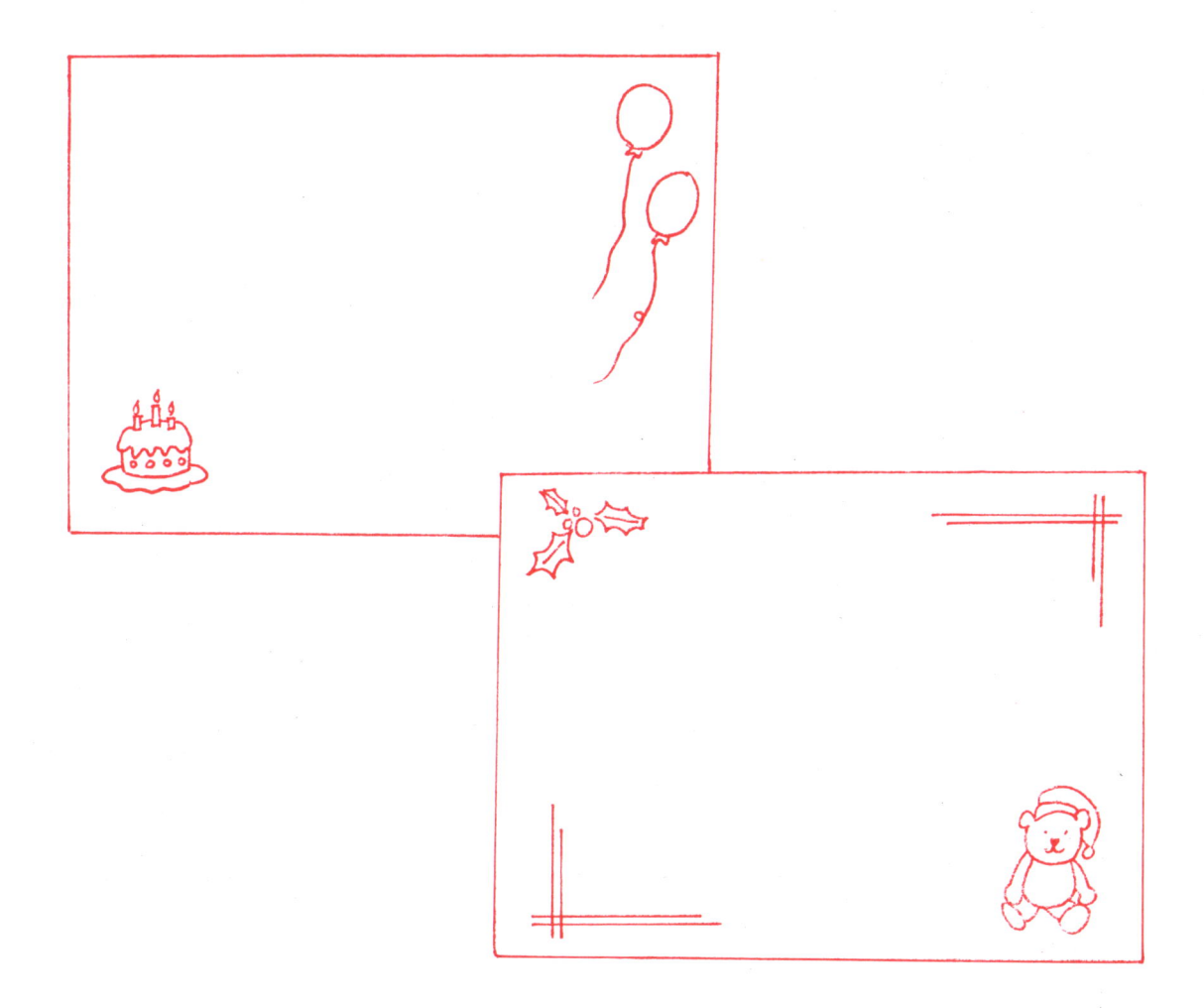

10 ORDERING FOOD

VOCABULARY

	Pinyin	Yale Lau	English
餃子	jiǎozi	gáau jí gaau² ji²	dumpling(s)
蝦餃	xiājiǎo	hà gáau ha¹ gaau²	prawn dumpling(s)
燒賣	sháomài	sìu máai siu¹ maai²	pork dumpling(s)
魚	yú	yùh yue⁴	fish
魚翅餃	yǔchi jiǎo	yùh chi gáau yue⁴ chi³ gaau²	shark fin dumpling(s)

飽	bāo	bàau baau¹	bun, bread
叉燒飽	chāshǎobāo	chà sìu bàau cha¹ siu¹ baau¹	BBQ pork bun
鳳爪	fèngzhǎo	fuhng jáau fung⁶ jaau²	Pheonix claw (chicken feet)
骨	gǔ	gwàt gwat¹	bone
排骨	páigǔ	pàaih gwàt paai⁴ gwat¹	spare rib
葉	yè	yihp yip⁶	leaf
牛	niú	ngàuh ngau⁴	cow
*牛栢(柏)葉	niúbóyè	ngàuh paak yihp ngau⁴ paak³ yip⁶	cow stomach
雞	jī	gài gai¹	chicken
珍珠	zhēnzhū	jàn jyù jan¹ jue¹	pearl
珍珠雞	zhēnzhūjī	jàn jyù gài jan¹ jue¹ gai¹	sticky rice chicken

USEFUL EXPRESSIONS

1. 請問有沒有……？   Please do you have (any) …?

    e.g. 請問有沒有蝦餃？

Pinyin: Qǐng wèn yǒu méi yǒu xiājiǎo?
Yale: Chíng mahn yáuh muht yáuh hà gáau?
Lau: Ching² man⁶ yau⁵ mut⁶ yau⁵ ha¹ gaau²?
English: Please do you have any prawn dumplings?

---

* 栢 is written in a colloquial way and 柏 is written in a formal way.

請問	有沒有	蝦餃 叉燒飽 排骨	?	Please	do you have (any)	prawn dumplings? BBQ Pork buns? spare ribs?

Response: *Pinyin*   *Yale/Lau*   *English*

有。	yǒu	yáuh yau5	Yes, (I have/do)
沒有。	méi yǒu	muht yáuh mut6 yau5	No, (I haven't/don't)

2. 對不起。

e.g. 對不起，我沒有蝦餃。

Sorry.
Pinyin: Duì bù qǐ, wǒ méi yǒu xiājiǎo.
Yale: Deui bàt héi, ngóh muht yáuh hà gáau.
Lau: Deui3 bat1 hei2, ngo5 mut6 yau5 ha1 gaau2.
English: Sorry, we don't have prawn dumplings.

3. 沒關係。

Pinyin: Méi guānxi.
Yale: Muht gwàan heih.
Lau: Mut6 gwaan1 hei6.
English: Never mind.

4. 謝謝。

Pinyin: xiè xie.
Yale: Jeh jeh.
Lau: Je6 je6.
English: Thanks. (often used in Putonghua. Cantonese use 多謝 dò jeh/do1 je6 or 唔該 ǹgh goih/ng4 goi6 to express thanks)

ADVERTISEMENT EXPLANATIONS

蝦餃、燒賣、魚翅餃、叉燒飽、鳳爪、排骨、牛栢葉、珍珠雞。

English:

Prawn dumplings, siu mai dumplings, sharp fin dumplings, barbeque pork buns, pheonix claws, spare ribs, cow stomach, sticky rice chicken. (Take the MTR and get to your dim sum quicker.)

Note:

Being able to order food is a very important survival skill in most Chinese speaking communities. In Hong Kong, it is vital that one is able to order food in a Dim Sum restaurant. Dim Sum is almost never eaten alone and your companions will be most appreciative of your abilities if you can order food for them.

Beware, however, for there are several pitfalls that stand in the way of you obtaining a feast: most Dim Sum carries exotic and expensive-sounding names such as "pheonix claw", "pearl chicken" and "shark fin." Many people are disappointed when their exotic menu turns into chicken feet, small pieces of chicken meat and vermicelli strands! The tonal system of Chinese can also stand between you and a heavenly repast. It is not unusual for learners in a restaurant to order ice-cream but to be presented with steaming coffee!

ACTIVITY 1

Write the Chinese characters.

ク 鱼 魚

| 魚 | | | | | | | | | | | |

虫 虾 蝦

| 蝦 | | | | | | | | | | | |

𠂉 牛

| 牛 | | | | | | | | | | | |

⺈ 乑 奚 奚 雞 雞

| 雞 | | | | | | | | | | | |

ACTIVITY 2

Write the number to show the order of the picture so that the conversations make sense to you.

| 1. 不要緊。 | 2. 請問有沒有蝦餃？ | 3. 對不起，我沒有蝦餃。 |

ACTIVITY 3

Match the animals with the suitable words.

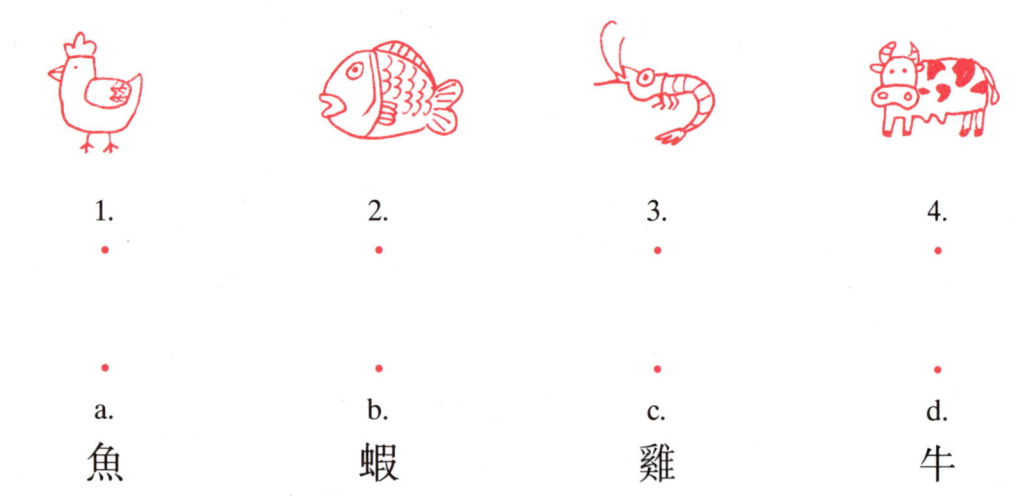

1.   2.   3.   4.

a. 魚   b. 蝦   c. 雞   d. 牛

ACTIVITY 4

Pair work—ordering food in a Chinese restaurant.

Student A should use the information below and student B should use the information on page 114.

Student A Worksheet: You would like to have the following dim sum. Ask the waiter/waitress to see if he/she has the food you want.

You can use these sentence patterns to help you.

> You: 請問有沒有……？
> Waiter: ……
> You: 謝謝。／不要緊。

11 FROM THE OCEAN TO THE SKY

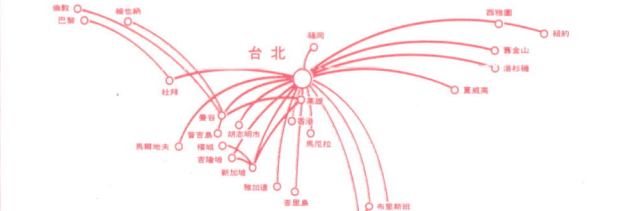

VOCABULARY

	Pinyin	Yale / Lau	English
海洋	hǎi yáng	hói yèuhng hoi² yeung⁴	ocean
天空	tiān kōng	tìn hùng tin¹ hung¹	sky
長榮航空	cháng róng háng kōng	Chèuhng Wìhng Hòhng Hùng Cheung⁴ Wing⁴ Hong⁴ Hung¹	Eva air
遠	yuǎn	yúhn yuen⁵	far
超過	chāo guò	chìu gwo chiu¹ gwoh³	beyond
期待	qī dài	kèih doih kei⁴ doi⁶	expectation
*與(＝和)	yǔ (hé)	yúh (wòh) yue⁵ (wo⁴)	and
想像	xiǎng xiàng	séung jeuhng seung² jeung⁶	imagination

SUPPLEMENTARY VOCABULARY

三歲	sān suì	sàam seui saam¹ seui³	3 years old, aged 3
年輕	niánqīng	nìhn hèng nin⁴ heng¹	young

USEFUL EXPRESSIONS

1. 從……到……。   from … (a place) to … (a place)

---

* 與 is used in formal writing, in speaking we use 和

63

e.g. 從沙田到九龍，只需 10 分鐘。

Pinyin: Cóng Shātián dào Jiǔlóng, zhǐ xū shí fēng zhōng.
Yale: Chùhng Sàtìhn dou Gáu Lùhng, jí sèui sahp fàn jùng.
Lau: Chung⁴ Sa¹ Tin⁴ do³ Gau² Lung⁴, ji² seui¹ sap⁶ fan¹ jung¹.
English: From Shatin to Kowloon, (it takes) only 10 minutes.

2. ……過……。

e.g. 我大過你。

Only used in Cantonese expressions, showing a comparison between two things.
Pinyin: Wǒ dà guò nǐ.
Yale: Ngóh daih gwo néih.
Lau: Ngo⁵ dai⁶ gwoh³ nei⁵.
English: I am bigger than you.
　　　　(also: I am older than you.)

我	大 過 高 過 重 過	你。

I (am)	older than taller than heavier than	you.

3. (person)……比(person)……大^(another)。

e.g. 我比你大。

Used in both Cantonese and Putongua to show a comparison between two things.
(比 = compare with)
Pinyin: Wǒ bǐ nǐ dà.
Yale: Ngóh béi néih daih.
Lau: Ngo⁵ bei² nei⁵ dai⁶.
English: I am bigger than you. (or: I am older than you.)

direct translation:

我 他 你	比	你 我 他	大。 高。 重。

I He You	compared with	you me him	big. tall. heavy.

4. (person)……比(person)……大^(another)(quantity)……。

(person) compared with (person)^(another) older than (quantity) e.g. 我比你大三歲。

Pinyin: Wǒ bǐ nǐ dà sān suì.
Yale: Ngóh béi néih daih sàam seui.
Lau: Ngo5 bei2 nei5 dai6 saam1 seui3.
English: I am 3 years older than you.

English:

我 他 你	比	你 我 他	大 3 歲。 年輕 1 歲。 重 2 磅。

I am He is You are	3 years older 1 year younger 2 lbs heavier	than	you. me. him.

direct translation:

I He You	compared with	you me him	bigger 3 years. younger 1 year. heavier 2 lbs.

5. ……與……

 (= ……和……)

 e.g. 我有一個橙和三個蘋果。

… and …

Pinyin: Wǒ yǒu yī gè chéng hé sān zhī píngguǒ.
Yale: Ngóh yáuh yàt go cháang wòh sàam jek pìhng gwó.
Lau: Ngo5 yau5 yat1 goh3 chaang2 wo4 saam1 goh3 ping4 gwo2.
English: I have one orange and three apples.

ADVERTISEMENT EXPLANATION

從海洋到天空
長榮航空遠超過你的期待與想像

Pinyin: Cóng hǎiyáng dào tiān kōng, Cháng Róng Háng Kōng yuǎn chāoguò nǐde qīdài yǔ xiǎnggxiàng.
Yale: Chùhng hói yeùhng dou tìn hùng, Chèuhng Wìhng Hòhng Hùng yúhn chìu gwo neíh dìk kèih doih yúh séung jeuhng.
Lau: Chung4 hoi2 yeung4 do3 tin1 hung1, Cheung4 Wing4 Hong4 Hung1 yun5 chiu1 gwoh3 nei5 dik1 kei4 doi6 yue5 seung jeung6.
English: From the ocean to the sky, Eva Air is far beyond your expectation and imagination.

ACTIVITY 1

Write the Chinese characters.

彳 伙 從

| 從 | | | | | | | | | | | |

厶 至 到

| 到 | | | | | | | | | | | |

冎 咼 咼 過

| 過 | | | | | | | | | | | |

臼 舁 舁 與

| 與 | | | | | | | | | | | |

千 禾 和

| 和 | | | | | | | | | | | |

氵 汁 洢 海 海 氵 氵 洋

| 海 | 洋 | | | | | | | | | | |

二 天 宀 穴 空

| 天 | 空 | | | | | | | | | | |

66

ACTIVITY 2

Pairwork—who is who?

Student A should use the information below and student B should use the information on page 115.

Worksheet A: Here are six people and some information about them.

| | | Bob | | | |

Bob 比 Sally 大一歲。

May 比 Judy 和 Sally 肥。

Joe 今年 21 歲。

最高的人比 Joe 年輕一歲。

Judy 最大——她比 May 大 4 歲。

Student B also has information about the six people. Work together to see if you can work out their names and their ages. Write them in the boxes.

You are allowed to read out the information you have about the six people but you must not let student B see your answer. For students who study individually: combine the information from A and B and work out the answers.

ACTIVITY 3

Indiana Jones Adventure

You are now in city A and your mission is to get the world's biggest diamond from F. There are several routes you can take but some bad guys are trying to get the diamond too. You have to be quick! Here is some information you need:

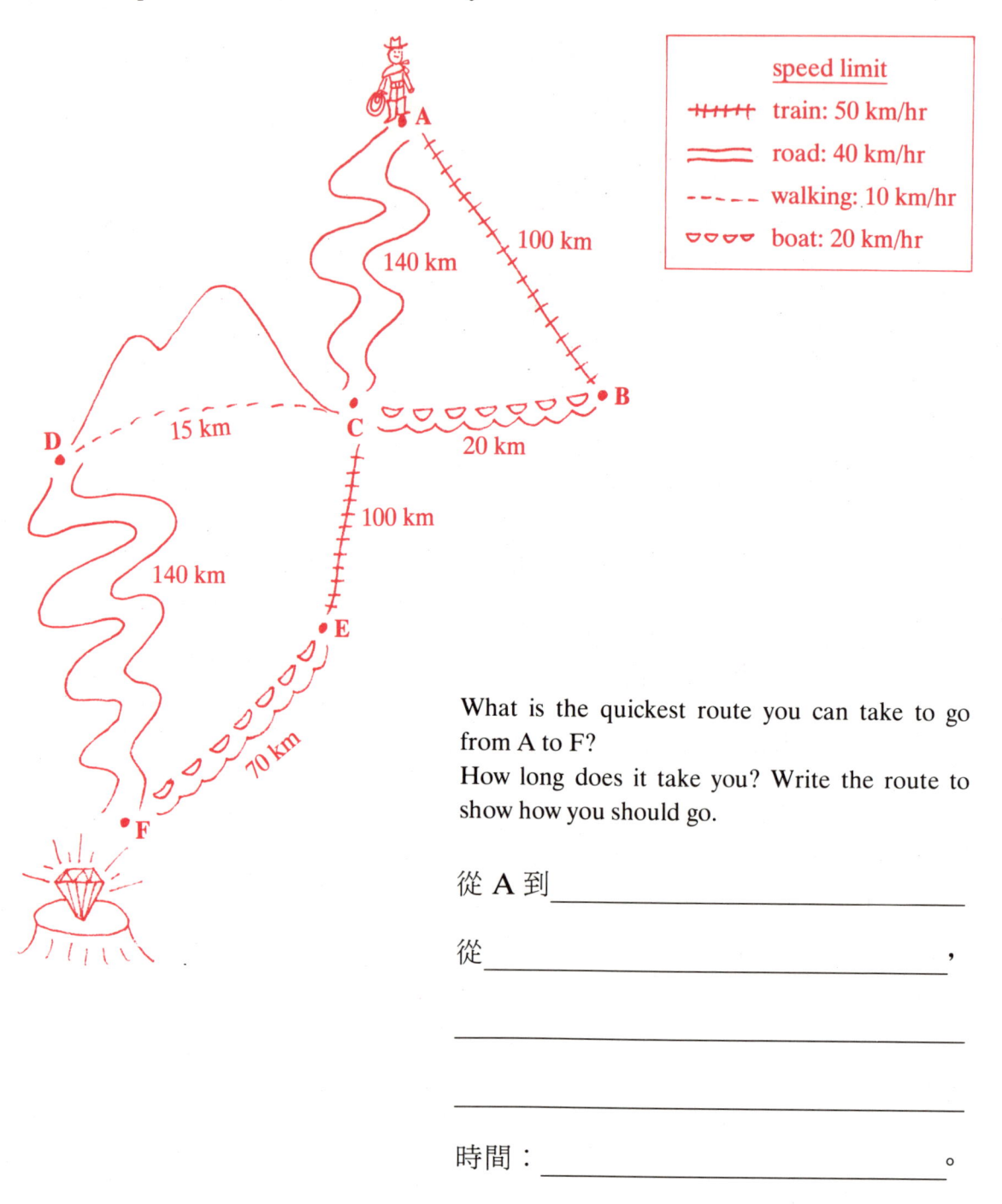

speed limit
- train: 50 km/hr
- road: 40 km/hr
- walking: 10 km/hr
- boat: 20 km/hr

A to C: road, 140 km
A to B: train, 100 km
B to C: boat, 20 km
C to D: walking, 15 km
C to E: train, 100 km
D to F: road, 140 km
E to F: boat, 70 km

What is the quickest route you can take to go from A to F?
How long does it take you? Write the route to show how you should go.

從 A 到＿＿＿＿＿＿＿＿＿＿＿＿＿＿＿＿

從＿＿＿＿＿＿＿＿＿＿＿＿＿＿＿＿＿＿，

＿＿＿＿＿＿＿＿＿＿＿＿＿＿＿＿＿＿＿

＿＿＿＿＿＿＿＿＿＿＿＿＿＿＿＿＿＿＿

時間：＿＿＿＿＿＿＿＿＿＿＿＿＿＿。

12 WHO COMES TO CARE ABOUT ME?

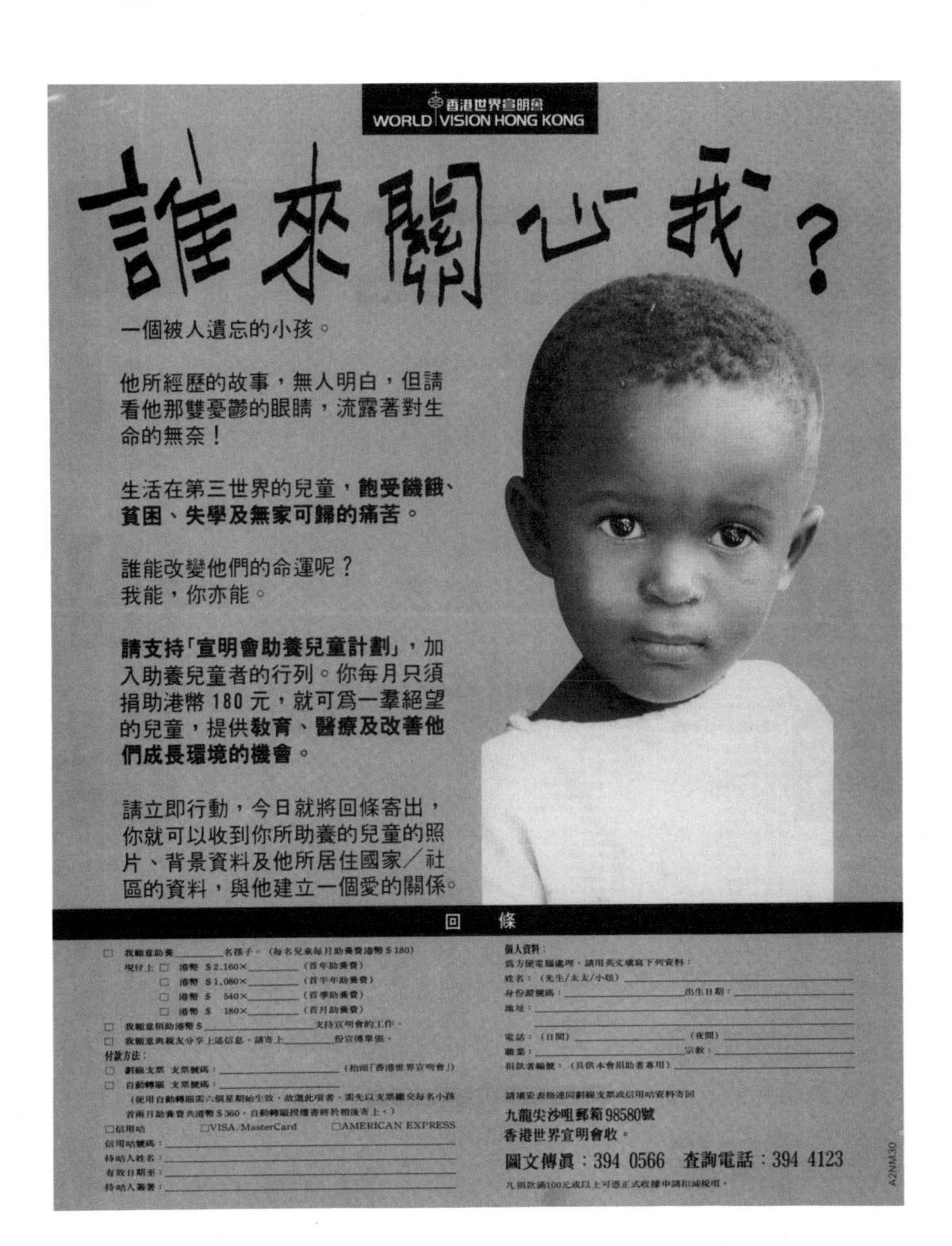

誰來關心我？

WORLD VISION HONG KONG 香港世界宣明會

一個被人遺忘的小孩。

他所經歷的故事，無人明白，但請看他那雙憂鬱的眼睛，流露著對生命的無奈！

生活在第三世界的兒童，**飽受饑餓、貧困、失學及無家可歸的痛苦。**

誰能改變他們的命運呢？
我能，你亦能。

請支持「宣明會助養兒童計劃」，加入助養兒童者的行列。你每月只須捐助港幣180元，就可為一羣絕望的兒童，提供**教育、醫療**及**改善他們成長環境的機會。**

請立即行動，今日就將回條寄出，你就可以收到你所助養的兒童的照片、背景資料及他所居住國家／社區的資料，與他建立一個愛的關係。

回條

☐ 我願意助養 _____ 名孩子。（每名兒童每月助養費港幣 $180）
現付上　☐ 港幣 $2,160× _____（首年助養費）
　　　　☐ 港幣 $1,080× _____（首半年助養費）
　　　　☐ 港幣 $ 540× _____（首季助養費）
　　　　☐ 港幣 $ 180× _____（首月助養費）
☐ 我願意捐助港幣 $ _____ 支持宣明會的工作。
☐ 我願意與親友分享上述信息，請寄上 _____ 份宣傳單張。

付款方法：
☐ 劃線支票　支票號碼：_____（抬頭「香港世界宣明會」）
☐ 自動轉賬　支票號碼：_____
（使用自動轉賬需六個星期始生效，故選此項者，需先以支票繳交每名小孩首월助養費共港幣 $360，自動轉賬授權者將於稍後寄上。）
☐ 信用咭　　☐ VISA/MasterCard　☐ AMERICAN EXPRESS
信用咭號碼：_____
持咭人姓名：_____
有效日期至：_____
持咭人簽署：_____

個人資料：
為方便電腦處理，請用英文填寫下列資料：
姓名：（先生/太太/小姐）_____
身份證號碼：_____ 出生日期：_____
地址：_____
電話：（日間）_____（夜間）_____
職業：_____ 宗教：_____
捐款者編號：_____（只供本會捐助者專用）

請填妥表格連同劃線支票或信用咭資料寄回

九龍尖沙咀郵箱98580號
香港世界宣明會收。

圖文傳真：394 0566　　查詢電話：394 4123

凡捐款滿100元或以上可憑正式收據申請扣減稅項。

VOCABULARY

	Pinyin	Yale / Lau	English
誰	shuí	sèuih / seui⁴	who
來	lái	lòih / loi⁴	come
關心	guānxīn	gwàan sàm / gwaan¹ sam¹	care

SUPPLEMENTARY VOCABULARY

	Pinyin	Yale / Lau	English
陳太太	Chén tàitai	Chàhn tai tái / Chan⁴ tai³ tai²	Mrs. Chan
陳先生	Chén xiānsheng	Chàhn sìn sàang / Chan⁴ sin¹ saang¹	Mr. Chan
陳小姐	Chén xiǎojie	Chàhn síu jé / Chan⁴ siu² je²	Miss Chan
過來	guòlái	gwo lòih / gwo³ loi⁴	come here
請	qǐng	chíng / ching²	please

USEFUL EXPRESSIONS

1. 你是誰？

Pinyin: Nǐ shì shuí?
Yale: Néih sih sèuih?
Lau: Nei⁵ si⁶ seui⁴?
English: You are who? (= Who are you?)

* direct translation

你 他 她	是	誰？

You He She	are is	who?

=

in English pattern

Who	are is	you? he? she?

note: 是誰？ = who is it?

2. 誰是……？

e.g. 誰是陳太太？

Who is …?
Pinyin: Shuí shì Chén tàitai?
Yale: Sèuih sih Chàhn tai tái?
Lau: Seui⁴ si⁶ Chan⁴ tai³ tai²?
English: Who is Mrs. Chan?

誰	是	你的老師？ 陳太太？ 他的妹妹？

Who	is	your teacher? Mrs. Chan? his sister?

3. 請過來。

Pinyin: Qǐng quòlái.
Yale: Chíng gwo lòih.
Lau: Ching² gwo³ loi⁴.
English: Please come here.

ADVERTISEMENT EXPLANATION

誰來關心我？

Pinyin: Shuí lái guānxīn wǒ?
Yale: Sèuih lòih gwàan sàm ngóh?
Lau: Seui⁴ loi⁴ gwaan¹ sam¹ ngoh⁵?
English: Who comes to care about me?

ACTIVITY 1

Write the Chinese characters.

言 訁 誰

誰											

十 中 來

來											

丨 門 閂 關 關 丶 心 心

關	心										

日 旦 是

是											

ACTIVITY 2

Choose and arrange the following tiles to form the sentences given in English below.

請 來 不 可 你 可 以 過 老 師

1. Come.

	。

2. Come here.

		。

3. Please come here.

			。

4. Teacher, please come here.

		,					。

5. Teacher, can you come here?

		,								。

ACTIVITY 3

This is a picture of Mary's family. She is describing her family members. Can you tell who she is talking about?

> 長頭髮的是我妹妹，我哥哥最高，媽媽最肥，我弟弟在打電話，我在吃東西。

Mary

1. 誰是 Mary 的媽媽？ _____

2. 誰是她的弟弟？ _____

3. 誰是她的哥哥？ _____

4. 誰是她的妹妹？ _____

5. 誰是 Mary？ _____

13 YOU ONLY NEED A STAMP

只需一個郵票，
即可坐遊
全澳洲！

VOCABULARY

	Pinyin	Yale / Lau	English
只需	zhǐ xū	jí sùi / yi[2] sui[1]	only need
郵票	yóupiào	yàuh piu / yau[4] piu[3]	stamp(s)

即	jí	jìk jik¹	immediately
可 (= 可以)	kě (kě yǐ)	hó (hó yíh) hoh² (hoh² yi⁵)	may, can, able to
坐	zuò	joh (chóh) joh⁶ (choh²)	sit
遊	yóu	yàuh yau⁴	travel
全	quán	chyùhn chuen⁴	all, whole
澳洲	Àozhōu	Ou jàu O³ jau¹	Australia

SUPPLEMENTARY VOCABULARY

國	guó	gwok gwok³	country
美國	Měiguó	Méi gwok Mei² gwok³	America
中國	Zhōngguó	Jùng gwok Jung¹ gwok³	China
英國	Yīngguó	Yìng gwok Ying¹ gwok³	England
美國人	Měiguó rén	Méi gwok yàhn Mei² gwok³ yan⁴	American
中國人	Zhōngguó rén	Jùng gwok yàhn Jung¹ gwok³ yan⁴	Chinese
英國人	Yīngguó rén	Yìng gwok yàhn Ying¹ gwok³ yan⁴	English/British
澳洲人	Àozhōu rén	Ou jàu yàhn O³ jau¹ yan⁴	Australian
法國人	Fǎguó rén	Faat gwok yàhn Faat³ gwok³ yan⁴	French

MEASURE WORD

一<u>個</u>郵票 yīge yóupiào   yàt go yàuh piu   a stamp
yat¹ goh³ yau⁴ piu³

USEFUL EXPRESSIONS

1. ……<u>只需</u>……。

e.g. 從香港到美國，<u>只需</u>八小時。

… only need … (it takes only …)

Pinyin: Cóng xiānggǎng dào Měiguó <u>zhǐ xū</u> bā shǎo shí
Yale: Chùhng Hèung Góng dou Méi Gwok, <u>jí sèui</u> baat síu sìh.
Lau: Chung⁴ Heung¹ Gong² do³ Mei² gwok³, <u>ji² seui¹</u> baat³ siu² si⁴.
English: From Hong Kong to America, (it takes) <u>only</u> eight hour.

2. (subject)<u>可以</u>(verb)。

e.g. 我<u>可以</u>唱歌。

… can/may …

Pinyin: Wǒ <u>kěyǐ</u> chànggē.
Yale: Ngóh <u>hó yíh</u> cheung gò.
Lau: Ngoh⁵ <u>hoh⁵ yi⁵</u> cheung³ goh¹
English: I <u>can</u> sing.

"can" pattern (showing ability)

我 他 她	可以	唱歌。 寫字。 講中文。

I He She	can	sing. write speak Chinese.

"may" pattern (giving permission)

你們 她 你	可以	坐下。 吃一個蘋果。 出去。

You She You	may	sit down. eat an apple. go out.

3. 我可不可以……？

(Asking for permission)
I may or may not …? (= May I…?)
I can or canot …? (= Can I…?)

e.g. 媽媽，我可不可以吃一個蘋果？

Pinyin: Māma, wǒ kě bù kěyǐ chī yīge píngguǒ?
Yale: Mà mà, ngóh hó bàt hó yíh hek yàt go pìhng gwó?
Lau: Ma¹ ma¹, ngoh⁵ hoh⁵ bat¹ hoh⁵ yi⁵ hek³ yat¹ goh³ ping⁴ gwo²?
English: Mother, May (Can) I eat an apple?

我	可不可以	吃蘋果？ 開窗？ 去洗手間？ 坐下？

May Can	I	eat an apple? open the window? go to the toilet? sit down?

Response:

可以	Yes, (you) can.
不可以	No, (you) can't.

ADVERTISEMENT EXPLANATION

只需一個郵票，即可坐遊全澳洲！

Pinyin: Zhǐ xū yīge yóupiào, jí kě zuò yóu quán Àozhōu.
Yale: Jí sùi yàt go yàuh piu, jìk hó joh jàuh chyùhn Ou jau.
Lau: Ji² sui¹ yat¹ goh³ yau⁴ piu³, jik¹ ho¹ joh⁶ yau⁴ chuen⁴ Ou³ jau¹.
English: (You) only need one stamp to immediately travel the whole of Australia.

ACTIVITY 1

Write the Chinese characters.

只 帀 需 需

只	需								

口 可 以 以

可	以										

ㅆ 坐 坐

坐											

氵 沪 澗 澳 氵 氵 洲 洲

澳	洲										

ACTIVITY 2

Label each of the following countries on the map.

1 澳洲   2 法國   3 美國   4 英國

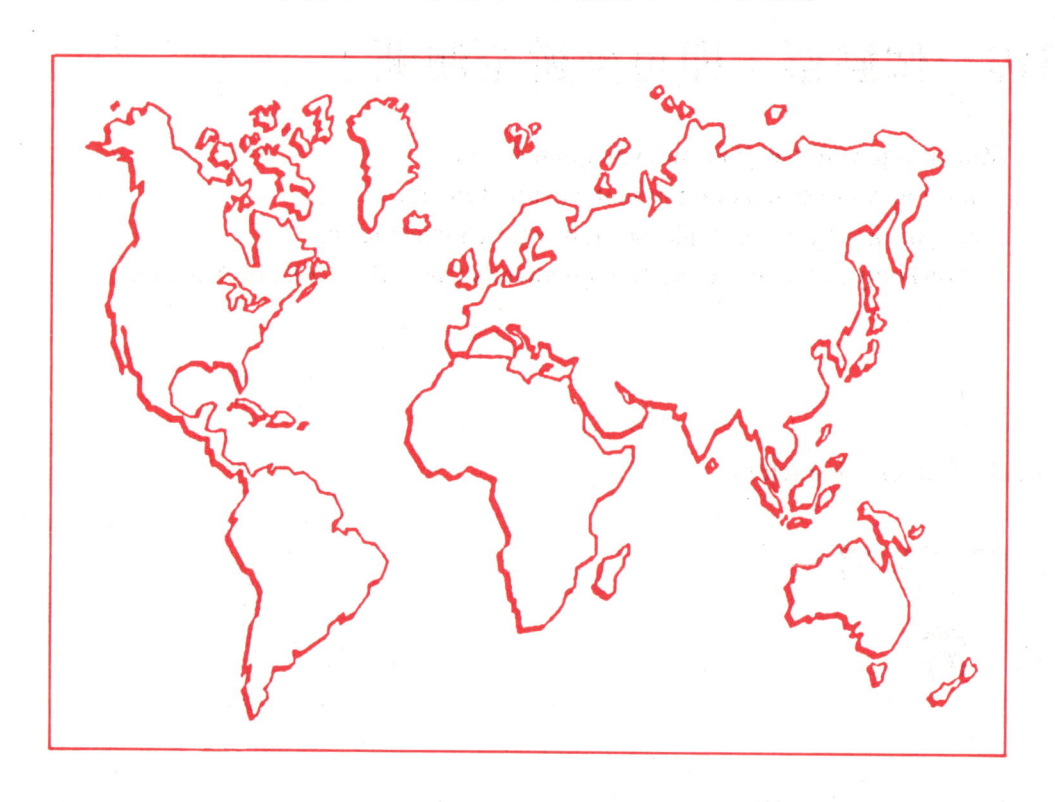

ACTIVITY 3

What nationality are these people?

e.g. 我是澳洲人。

1.  我是 ☐ ☐ ☐ 。

2. 我是 ☐ ☐ ☐ 。

3. 我是 ☐ ☐ ☐ 。

ACTIVITY 4

Peter is sick in the hospital. There is a card showing what he can do ☑ and cannot do ☒. His mother has come to visit him and she has lots of questions to ask. Answer her questions according to the card by writing "可以" or "不可以".

☒ drink tea
☑ sit
☒ go to toilet
☑ eat fruit

1. Peter 可不可以吃蘋果？
_____

2. 他可不可以喝茶？
_____

3. 他可不可以坐？
_____

4. 他可不可以去洗手間？
_____

14　LONG, SMALL AND EASY

220分鐘通話時間　　優點一望就知

MOBILE PHONES BY ERICSSON

如欲索取詳盡資料，請親往和記電訊、和記電話、香港電訊、訊聯網絡或數碼通各門市部查詢。

攜帶方便收藏易　　全憑一個字

MOBILE PHONES BY ERICSSON

如欲索取詳盡資料，請親往和記電訊、和記電話、香港電訊、訊聯網絡或數碼通各門市部查詢。

功能全面顯示　　結果只得一個字

MOBILE PHONES BY ERICSSON

如欲索取詳盡資料，請親往和記電訊、和記電話、香港電訊、訊聯網絡或數碼通各門市部查詢。

VOCABULARY

	Pinyin	Yale / Lau	English
分鐘	fēnzhōng	fàn jùng / fan¹ jung¹	minute(s)
通話	tōnghuà	tùng wah / tung¹ wa⁶	conversation (through telephone)
時間	shíjiān	sìh gaan / si⁴ gaan³	time
優點	yōudiǎn	yàu dím / yau¹ dim²	merit
一望就知	yī wàng jiù zhī	yàt mohng jauh jì / yat¹ mong⁶ jau⁶ ji¹	know it at a quick glance
攜帶	xiédài	kwàih daai / kwai⁴ daai³	carry
方便	fāngbiàn	fòng bihn / fong¹ bin⁶	convenient
收藏	shōucáng	sàu chòhng / sau¹ chong⁴	keep, store
易(容易)	yì (róng yì)	yih (yùhng yih) / yi⁶ (yung⁴ yi⁶)	easy
全憑	quán píng	chyùhn pàhng / chuen⁴ pang⁴	all depend/rely on
功能	gōngnéng	gùng nàhng / gung¹ nang⁴	function(s)
全面	quán miàn	chyùhn mihn / chuen⁴ min⁶	completely
顯示	xiǎnshì	hín sih / hin² si⁶	show, depict
結果	jiéguǒ	git gwó / git³ gwo²	result, outcome

只得 (＝只有)	zhǐde (zhǐyou)	jí dàk (jí yáuh) ji² dak¹ (ji² yau⁵)	only have, have nothing but
細(＝細小)	xì (xìxiǎo)	sai (sai síu) sai³ (sai³ siu²)	small
長	cháng	chèuhng cheung⁴	long

MEASURE WORD

一<u>個</u>字	yī gè zì	yàt go jih yat¹ goh³ ji⁶	one word

USEFUL EXPRESSIONS

There are several ways to make interrogative sentences in Chinese. Two of which are:

a. using affirmative-negative question form:

   e.g. ……長不長？……大不大？……高不高？

b. using modal particle 嗎 (mā, mà, ma¹) at the end of the sentence:

   e.g. ……長嗎？……大嗎？……高嗎？

1. (something)……長不長？

   e.g. 她的頭髮長不長？

Is (Are) … long? (affirmative-negative form)

Pinyin: Tā de tóu fà cháng bù cháng?
Yale: Tà dìk tàuh faat chèuhng bàt chèuhng?
Lau: Ta¹ dik¹ tau⁴ faat³ cheung⁴ bat¹ cheung⁴?
English: Is her hair long?

她的頭髮 他 這本書 這間公司	長不長？ 高不高？ 重不重？ 大不大？	(Is) her hair (Is) he (Is) this book (Is) this company	long or not? tall or not? heavy or not? big or not?

Response:

長。 高。 重。 大。	Yes.	不長。 不高。 不重。 不大。	No.

2. ....長嗎？   Is (Are) ... long? (using modal particle 嗎 form)

   e.g. 她的頭髮長嗎？

   Pinyin: Tā de tóu fà cháng mā?
   Yale: Tà dìk tàuh faat chèunhg mà?
   Lau: Ta¹ dik¹ tau⁴ faat³ cheung⁴ ma¹?
   English: Is her hair long?

   * direct translation

她的頭髮	長	嗎？
他	高	
這本書	重	
這間公司	大	
你	好	

Her hair (is)	long?
He (is)	tall?
This book (is)	heavy?
This company (is)	big?
You (are)	well?
	(= How are you?)

ADVERTISEMENT EXPLANATION

220 分鐘通話時間，優點一望就知：長
攜帶方便收藏易，全憑一個字：細
功能全面顯示，結果只得一個字：易

Pinyin: Èr bǎi èr shí fēnzhōng tōnghuà shíjiān, yōudiǎn yī wàng jiù zhī: cháng.
    Xiédài fāngbiàn shōucáng yì, quán píng yī gè zì: xì.
    Gōngnéng quánmiàn xiǎnshì, jiéguǒ zhǐ dé yī gè zì: yì.
Yale: Yih bak yih sahp fàn jùng tùng wah sih gaan, yàu dím yàt mohng jauh jì: chèuhng.
    Kwàih daai fòng bìhn sàu chòhng yih, chyùhn pàhng yàt go jih: sai.
    Gùng nàhng chyùhn mihn hín sih, git gwó jí dak yàt go jih: yih.
Lau: Yi⁶ bak³ yi⁶ sap⁶ fan¹ jung¹ tung¹ wa⁶ si⁴ gaan³, yau¹ dim² yat¹ mong⁶ jau⁶ ji¹: cheung⁴.
    Kwai⁴ daai³ fong¹ bin⁶ sau¹ chong⁴ yi⁶, chuen⁴ pang⁴ yat¹ goh³ ji: sai³.
    Gung¹ nang⁴ chuen⁴ min⁶ hin² si⁶, git³ gwo² ji² dak¹ yat¹ goh³ ji: yi⁶.
English: 220 minutes conversation time, (you know) the merit at a glance: long.
    Convenient to carry, easy to keep, all depends on one word: small.
    It shows all the functions, the result is only one word: easy.

ACTIVITY 1

Write the Chinese characters.

厂 丨 長 長

| 長 | | | | | | | | | | | |

幺 糸 細

| 細 | | | | | | | | | | | |

日 昜 易

| 易 | | | | | | | | | | | |

吓 吗 嗎 嗎

| 嗎 | | | | | | | | | | | |

一 ア 不

| 不 | | | | | | | | | | | |

一 亻 们 個 個 宀 字

| 一 | 個 | 字 | | | | | | | | | |

日 旷 時 尸 門 間

| 時 | 間 | | | | | | | | | | |

ACTIVITY 2

Choose the picture that correctly describes the word.

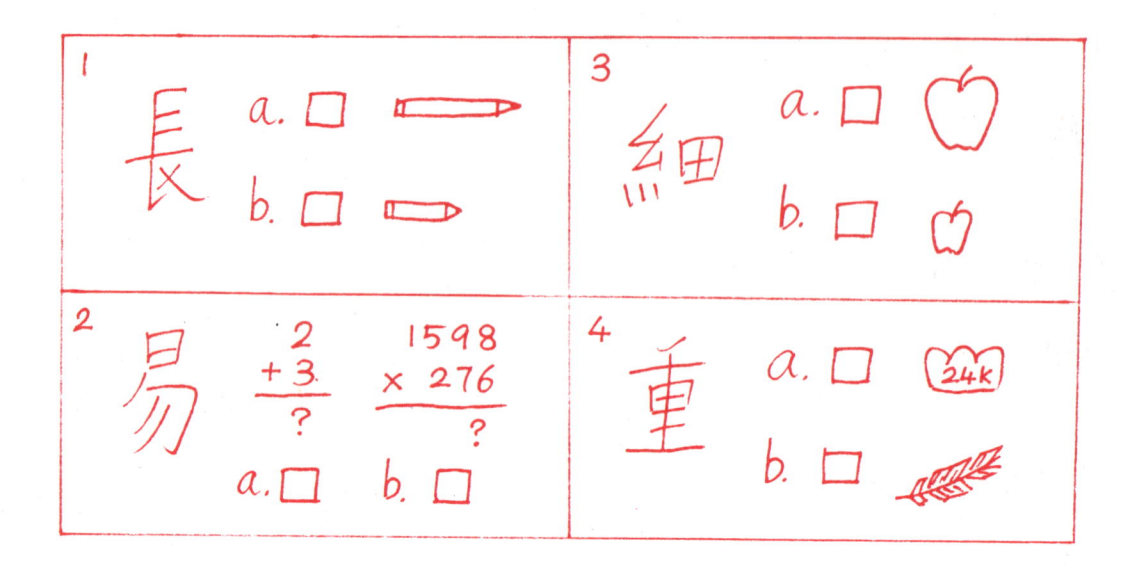

1. 長 a. ☐ (long pencil) b. ☐ (short pencil)
2. 易 a. ☐ 2+3=? b. ☐ 1598×276=?
3. 細 a. ☐ (big apple) b. ☐ (small apple)
4. 重 a. ☐ 24k (gold) b. ☐ (feather)

ACTIVITY 3

What are these people saying? Use 嗎 to help you finish their conversation.

e.g. 你愛我嗎？ 我愛你。

1. ☐☐☐☐☐☐？ 這書是我的。

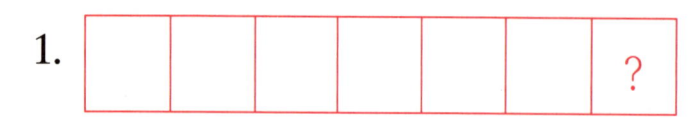

2. ☐☐☐☐☐☐☐☐?

她是我的妹妹。

3. ☐☐☐☐?

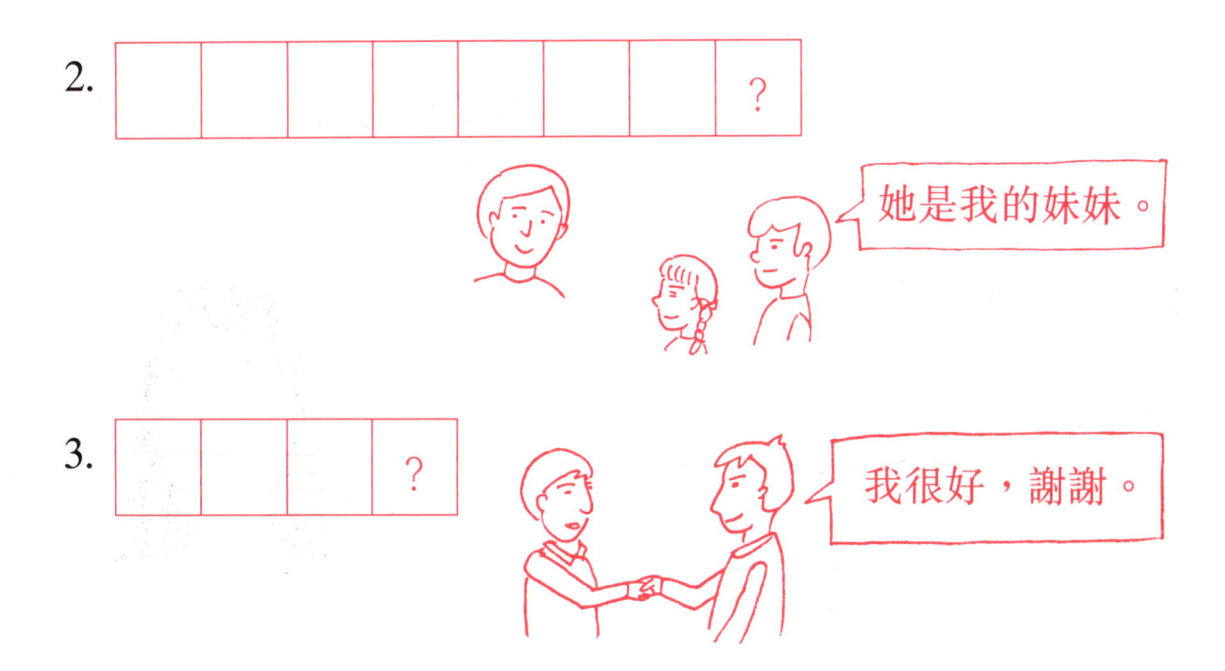

我很好，謝謝。

ACTIVITY 4

Pair Work—which one is the robber?
Student A should use the following information and Student B should turn to page 116.

Student A: The police are after a robber. You are a policeman. Here is the conversation between you and a witness (Student B)

Here are some of the questions you may ask:
Police: 他頭髮長不長？
Witness: …
Police: 口大不大？
Witness: …
Police: 鼻子長嗎？
Witness: …
Police: 他肥不肥胖？
Witness: …
Police: 眼大嗎？
Witness: …

a.

b.

c.

d.

Answer: Number ☐ is the robber.

If you do not know the answer, you may say:

不知道 bù zhīdào, bàt jì dou, bat¹ ji¹ do³, I don't know

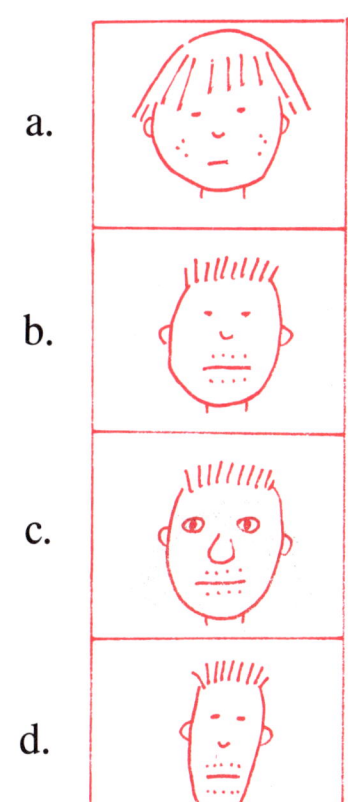

87

15 WE NEVER TREAT ANYBODY EQUALLY

無論黃種人、白種人或黑種人，你都擁有自己獨有的皮膚性質，而皮膚亦會隨年齡、氣候、環境或荷爾蒙分泌的變化，而受到不同程度的影響。要徹底護膚療膚，讓皮膚得到體貼照顧，我們能為你提供一個有效而又絕對「個人化」的辦法。

我們的每一個客人都會獲得不一樣的對待，因為我們能根據你的皮膚特性和需要，為你調配一套完全屬於自己的護膚品。

一般護膚品，只將皮膚分為中性、乾性、油性及混合性四種，忽略了各種皮膚的實際需要，而未能對症下藥；加上一般人對自己的皮膚性質缺乏認識，往往在護膚時未能達到理想效果。

PRESCRIPTION PLUS配護美護膚療膚系列，由美國美容學會融匯歐洲傳統護膚之道及美國皮膚護理的高科技，經十多年的研究，創製而成，並提出獨有的「個人調配」專業護膚新概念。

我們的專業美容師會為你先作詳盡皮膚分析，深入了解你的生活習慣、健康狀況及遺傳因素等，然後掌握你的皮膚需要，從我們的基本產品及附加精華素中，準確調配個別的護膚配方，成為你的皮膚獨享的護膚品。

PRESCRIPTION PLUS配護美護膚療膚系列，備有百多種基本產品及附加精華素，我們還會陸續研究更多新原素，全部純天然物質製造，配搭無窮無盡，無論任何一種皮膚，也可獲得更週全更體貼的照顧。

要你的皮膚得到真正呵護，我們絕不能一視同仁。若要親身享受配護美不一樣的體貼呵護，請即親臨或致電我們的：

調配中心：
香港中環太古大廈地下中央商場11室
電話：877 0778
九龍尖沙咀海洋中心商場251室
電話：922 63633
療膚中心：
香港中環德己立街1號世紀廣場3樓301室　電話：922 12791
九龍尖沙咀海洋中心9樓925室
電話：922 63063

面對不同
的客人
我們絕對不會
一視同仁

Prescription Plus
Clinical Skin Care™

VOCABULARY

	Pinyin	*Yale* *Lau*	*English*
面對	miàn duì	mihn deui min6 deui3	face (as a verb)
不同	bù tóng	bàt tùhng bat1 tung4	not the same (different)
客人	kèrén	haak yàhn haak3 yan4	guest(s), client(s)
絕對	juéduì	jyuht deui juet6 deui3	absolutely
不會	bùhuì	bàt wúih bat1 wooi5	never, will not
一視同仁	yīshìtóngrén	yàt sih tùhng yàhn yat1 si6 tung4 yan4	treat everyone equally

SUPPLEMENTARY VOCABULARY

游泳	yóuyǒng	yàuh wihng yau4 wing6	swim (verb) swimming (noun)
相同	xiāngtóng	seùng tùhng seung1 tung4	the same

USEFUL EXPRESSIONS

1. (someone) 會 (verb) — ... know how to, can, able to, will ... (expressing ability to do something)

   (someone) 不會 (verb) — ... do not know how to, cannot, unable to, will not ... (expressing inability to do something)

   e.g. 我會(不會)游泳。

   Pinyin: Wǒ huì (bù huì) yóu yǒng.
   Yale: Ngóh wúih (bàt wúih) yàuh wihng.
   Lau: Ngoh5 wooi5 (bat1 wooi5) yau4 wing6.
   English: I know (don't know) how to swim.

| 你
他
她 | 會 | 游泳。
唱歌。
寫字。 |

| I
He
She | know(s) how to
(can, be able to) | swim.
sing.
write. |

| 我
他
她 | 不會 | 游泳。
唱歌。
寫字。 |

| I
He
She | do/does not know how to
(cannot, be unable to) | swim.
sing.
write. |

2. 你會不會……？

e.g. 你<u>會不會</u>游泳？

Can you …?
Do you know how to …?

Pinyin: Nǐ <u>huì bùhuì</u> yóu yǒng?
Yale: Néih <u>wúih bàt wúih</u> yàuh wihng?
Lau: Nei5 <u>wooi5 bat1 wooi5</u> yau4 wing6?
English: <u>Can</u> you swim?

*direct translation   * in English pattern

| 你
他
她 | 會不會 | 游泳？
唱歌？
寫字？ |

| You
He
She | can or cannot | swim?
sing?
write? | = | Can you swim?
Can he sing?
Can she write? |

ADVERTISEMENT EXPLANATION

面對不同的客人，我們絕對不會一視同仁。

Pinyin: Miàn duì bù tóng de kērén, wǒmen juéduì bùhuì yīshì tóng rén.
Yale: Mihn dui bàt tùhng dìk haak yàhn, ngóh mùhn jyuht deui bàt wúih yàt sīh tùhng yàhn.
Lau: Min6 deui3 bat1 tung4 dik1 haak3 yan4, ngoh5 moon4 juet6 deui3 bat1 wooi5 yat1 si6. tung4 yan4.
English: (When) facing different clients, we absolutely never treat everybody equally.

ACTIVITY 1

Write the Chinese characters.

丆 面 面 ⺍ 芈 對

| 面 | 對 | | | | | | | | | |

不 丆 同
| 不 | 同 | | | | | | | | | | |

宀 㝏 客 客人
| 客 | 人 | | | | | | | | | | |

不 へ 侖 侖 會
| 不 | 會 | | | | | | | | | | |

ACTIVITY 2

Spot the differences. 有什麼不同？

Miss Chan has had plastic surgery and what a difference it has made!

What is different after her plastic surgery? Write 相同 (the same) in the blank if it is the same and write 不同 (not the same) in the blank if it is different.

1. 陳小姐的眼 → _____

2. 她的鼻子 → _____

3. 她的口 → _____

4. 她的頭髮 → _____

5. 她的面 → _____

Before

After

91

ACTIVITY 3

The following is a conversation between you, an interviewer and an interviewee in a survey. Read the conversation and fill in the survey form.

You: 請問你會不會游泳？

interviewee: 不會。

You: 你會不會唱歌？

interviewee: 會。

You: 你會不會做餅？

interviewee: 不會。

You: 你會不會寫中文字？

interviewee: 會。

You: 謝謝你。

interviewee: 不用謝。

Survey

Put a '✗' or a '✓' in the boxes below, depending on the answers to the questions.

Abilities:

☐ sing

☐ swim

☐ write Chinese

☐ make cakes

ACTIVITY 4

Do a small survey to find out how many people you know can sing, swim, write Chinese and make cakes. Draw a histogram to show your result. You can use the following question pattern to ask your friends:

你會不會唱歌？

人

唱歌　游泳　寫中文字　做餅

16 YELLOW PAGES

打開黃頁，
全港98間 除蟲
服務公司全部齊列. 〈圖中此類例外〉

VOCABULARY

	Pinyin	Yale Lau	English
除	chú	chèuih cheui⁴	cancel, remove
蟲	chóng	chùhng chung⁴	worm, bug
打	dǎ	dá da²	hit, beat
開	kāi	hòi hoi¹	open
黃頁	huáng yè	wohng yihp wong⁶ yip⁶	yellow page
全部	quánbù	chyùhn bouh chuen⁴ bo⁶	the whole
港	Gǎng	Góng Gong²	harbour (refer to Hong Kong)
服務	fúwù	fuhk mouh fuk⁶ mo⁶	service
公司	gōngsī	gùng sì gung¹ si¹	company
齊	qí	chàih chai⁴	complete, tidy
列	liè	liht lit⁶	list

SUPPLEMENTARY VOCABULARY

紅	hóng	hùhng hung⁴	red
綠	lǜ	luhk luk⁶	green
藍	lán	làahm laam⁴	blue

黑	hēi	hàk hak¹	black
白	bái	baahk baak⁶	white
門	mén	mùhn moon⁴	door
窗	chuāng	chèung cheung¹	window
百貨公司	bǎi huò gōngsī	baak fo gùng sì baak³ foh³ gung¹ si¹	Department Store
這裏(裡)	zhèli	jé léuih je² leui⁵	here
那裏	nàli	náh léuih na⁵ leui⁵	there
朋友	péngyou	pàhng yáuh pang⁴ yau⁵	friend(s)

MEASURE WORD

一間公司	yī jiān gōng sī	yàt gàan gùng sì yat¹ gaan¹ gung¹ si¹	a company

USEFUL EXPRESSIONS

1. 不要(verb phrase)……！   Don't …!

   e.g. 不要開門！

   Pinyin: Bùyào kái mén!
   Yale: Bàt yiu hòi mùhn!
   Lau: Bat¹ yiu³ hoi¹ moon⁴!
   English: Don't open the door!

不要	開	門。 窗。 燈。

Don't	open	the door. the window. the light.*

*note: 開 "open" has the same meaning as "switch on" or "turn on". In Chinese, we can "open the light", "open the fan", "open the television", etc.

2. (noun phrase) 全(部)都是 (noun)。　　… all are…

Pinyin: Tāmen quán dōu shi xiǎo hái zǐ.
Yale: Tà mùhn chyùhn dòu sih síu hàih jí.
Lau: Ta¹ moon⁴ chun⁴ dou¹ si⁶ siu² hai⁴ ji².
English: They are all small children.

e.g. 他們全都是小孩子。

他們 這裏 她們	全(部)都是	小孩子。 男孩子。 女孩子。
那裏		你的東西。
這		我的。

They Here They	are all	small children. boys. girls.
There		your things.
These		mine.

ADVERTISEMENT EXPLANATION

除　蟲

Pesticide
The Chinese language is at times remarkably imaginative—instead of chicken feet one eats phoenix claws, for instance. At other times, the language is rather prosaic. Such is the case here: the word for pesticide literally translates to "remove worms"!
Whereas old-style Chinese is replete with imaginative words and phrases, words coined in more recent times are often more pragmatic and therefore rather lifeless in comparison. Such words are often simple juxtapositions of descriptions: telephone ("electric talk") is one such example, airplane ("flying machine") is another, and of course pesticide is a further example.

打開黃頁，全港 98 間服務公司全部齊列。
(圖中此類例外)

Pinyin: Dǎkāi huángyè, quán Gǎng jiǔ shí bā jiān fúwù gōngsī quánbù qíliè.
Yale: Dá hòi wòhng yihp, chyùhn Góng gáu sahp baat gàan fuhk mouh gùng sì chyùhn bouh chàih liht.
Lau: Da² hoi¹ wong⁶ yip⁶, chuen⁴ Gong² gau² sap⁶ baat³ gaan¹ fuk⁶ mo⁶ gung¹ si¹ chuen⁴ bo⁶ chai⁴ lit⁶.
English: (When you) open the Yellow Pages, 98 service companies in Hong Kong are all completely listed. (except for the kind shown in the picture below.)

ACTIVITY 1

Write the Chinese characters.

ㅋ 尸 門 閂 開

| 開 | | | | | | | | | | | |

艹 丗 苗 黃 厂 页 頁

| 黃 | 頁 | | | | | | | | | | |

八 公 ㄱ 司

| 公 | 司 | | | | | | | | | | |

入 全 立 音 部

| 全 | 部 | | | | | | | | | | |

ACTIVITY 2

Pyramid drill—read the following phrases carefully.

公司　　　　　　　　　　　　　　　company
服務公司　　　　　　　　　　　　service company
98 間服務公司　　　　　　　　　98 service companies
全港 98 間服務公司　　　　　　98 service companies in Hong Kong
全港 98 間服務公司齊列。　　98 service companies in Hong Kong are completely listed.
全港 98 間服務公司全部齊列。 98 service companies in Hong Kong are all completely listed.

Now use the same pattern with 百貨公司 (department store) to make the similar drill.

department store
38 department stores
38 department stores in HK
38 department stores in HK are completely listed.
38 department stores in HK are all completely listed.

百貨公司

_____

_____

_____

_____

ACTIVITY 3

What would you say in the following situation?

> 不要開門！　不要開燈！　不要開窗！

1.	2.	3.
！	！	！

ACTIVITY 4

Add "全都" (all are) to each sentence to make the sentence more widely applicable.

e.g. 他們是小孩子。　　　　　　(They are small children.)

他們<u>全都</u>是小孩子。　　　　(They are <u>all</u> small children.)

1. 這是我的東西。

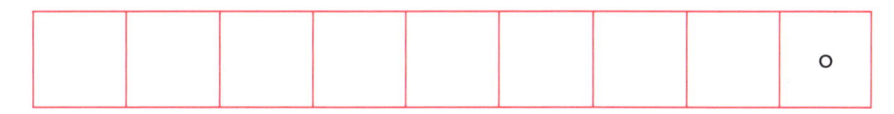

2. 那是我的書。

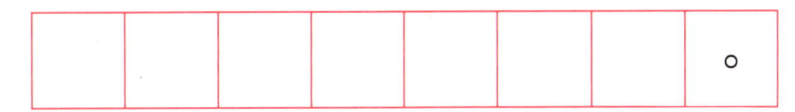

3. 她們是我的朋友。

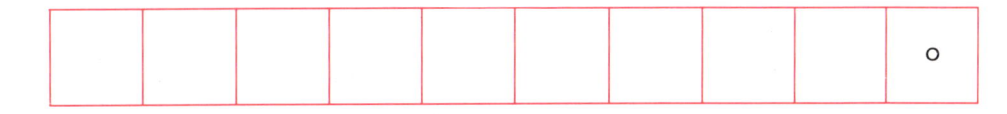

ACTIVITY 5

Match the colour with the correct Chinese word.

1. red　　•　　　　• a. 黑

2. green　•　　　　• b. 白

3. blue　 •　　　　• c. 綠

4. black　•　　　　• d. 紅

5. white　•　　　　• e. 藍

ACTIVITY 6

It is party time!
Pair Work—Student A should use the following information and student B should turn to page 116.
Listen to your partner's description and colour your mask accordingly.
Tell your partner the following description so that he/she can paint the right colour according to your instruction, too.

> 紅色的頭髮。
>
> 藍色的眼。
>
> 黑色的鼻子。
>
> 綠色的耳。
>
> 白色的口。

ACTIVITY 7

Colour the picture according to the following instructions.

> 蘋果全都是紅色。
>
> 杯子全都是藍色。
>
> 兩本書是黑色。
>
> 餅全都是綠色。

17 WHAT KIND OF THINGS?

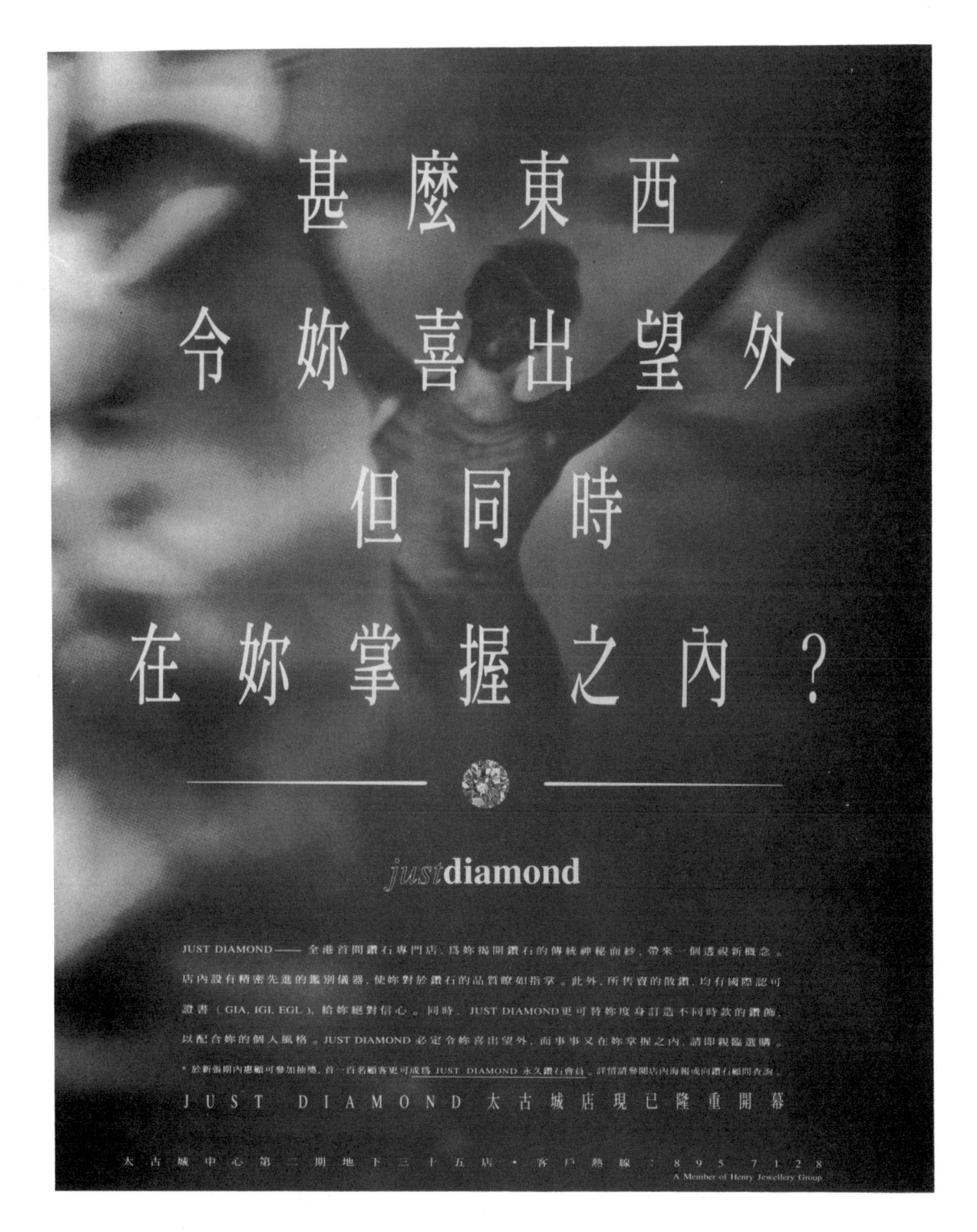

VOCABULARY

	Pinyin	Yale Lau	English
甚麼 (＝什麼)	shenmó	sahm mò sam6 mo1	what
東西	dōngxi	dùng sài dung1 sai1	thing
喜	xǐ	héi hei2	happy
出	chū	chèut cheut1	out
望	wàng	mohng mong6	look
外	wài	ngoih ngoi6	outside, out
喜出望外	xǐ chū wàng wài	héi chèut mohng ngoih hei2 cheut1 mong6 ngoi6	a very happy surprise
同時	tóngshí	tùhng sìh tung4 si4	at the same time
在	zài	joih joi6	in
掌握之內	zhǎngwò zhī nèi	jéung àak jì noih jeung2 aak1 ji1 noi6	within control
*妳	nǐ	neíh nei5	you (female)

---

* It is not common to use 妳 to describe female "you". It is now more common to use 你 "you" to describe both male or female.

SUPPLEMENTARY VOCABULARY

東面	dōngmiàn	dùng minh dung¹ min⁶	east side
南	nán	nàahm naam⁴	south
西	xī	sài sai¹	west
北	běi	bàk bak¹	north
上	shàng	seuhng seung⁶	up, on top
下	xià	hah ha⁶	down, below, bottom

USEFUL EXPRESSIONS

1. 甚麼東西……？

    e.g. 甚麼東西是圓的？

    What (kind) of thing (is) …?
    Pinyin: Shenmó dōngxi shi yuánde?
    Yale: Sahm mò dùng sài sih yùhn dìk?
    Lau: Sam⁶ mo¹ dung¹ sai¹ si⁶ yuen⁴ dik¹?
    English: What kind of thing is round?

2. (person) 令 (我) (adjective)

    e.g. 她令我開心。

    … make (me) …
    Pinyin: Tā lìng wǒ kāi xīn.
    Yale: Tà lihng ngóh hòi sàm.
    Lau: Ta¹ ling⁶ ngo⁵ hoi¹ sam¹.
    English: She makes me happy.

3. (noun) 在哪兒？

    e.g. 我的書在哪兒？

    Where is …?
    Pinyin: Wǒ de shū zài nǎer?
    Yale: Ngóh dìk sỳu joih náh yìh?
    Lau: Ngo⁵ dik¹ sue¹ joi⁶ na⁵ yi⁴?
    English: My book is where? (= Where is my book?)

4. (noun) 在 (a place)

    e.g. 你的書在枱上。

    (在 is used to show position: at, in, on, etc.)
    Pinyin: Nǐ de shū zài tái shàng.
    Yale: Néih dìk sỳu joih tói seuhng.
    Lau: Nei⁵ dik¹ sue¹ joi⁶ toi² seung⁶.
    English: Your book (is) on the table.

媽媽 爸爸 月兒 書	在	家。 公司。 天空。 枱上。
洗手間		東面。

Mother Father The moon The book	(is) at, in, on, etc.	home. work. the sky. the table.
The toilet		the east.

5. (subject)......在..........(verb phrase)

e.g. 我在看書。

(在 shows a present tense action: verb to be + ing)
Pinyin: Wǒ zài kàn shū.
Yale: Ngóh joih hon syù.
Lau: Ngo5 joi6 hon3 sue1.
English: I am reading a book.

我 太太 他	在	看書。 唱歌。 學鋼琴。

I (My) wife He	verb to be *(is, am, are, was, were)*	reading. singing. learning piano.

6. 你在做甚麼？

Pinyin: Nǐ zài zuò shenmó?
Yale: Néih joih jouh sahm mò?
Lau: Nei5 joi6 joi6 sam6 mo1?
English: You are doing what? (= What are you doing?)

你 她 老師 妹妹	在	做	甚麼？

You She The teacher (My) sister	is, are	doing	what?

ADVERTISEMENT EXPLANATION

甚麼東西令妳喜出望外，
但同時在妳掌握之內？

Pinyin: Shenmó dōngxi lìng nǐ xǐ chū wàng wài, dàn tóngshí zài nǐ zhǎngwò zhī nèi?
Yale: Sahm mò dùng sài lihng néih héi chèut mohng ngoih, daahn tùhng sìh joih néih jéung aak jì noih?

Lau: Sam⁶ mo¹ dung¹ sai¹ ling⁶ nei⁵ hei² cheut¹ mong⁶ ngoi⁶, daan⁶ tung⁴ si⁴ joi⁶ nei⁵ jeung² aak¹ ji¹ noi⁶?

English: What kind of thing can make you extremely happy, but at the same time within your control?

ACTIVITY 1

Write the Chinese characters.

甘 其 甚 广 麻 麼

甚	麼									

日 申 東 冂 西 西

東	西									

人 今 令

令										

冂 同 日 旷 時

同	時									

ナ 才 存 在

在										

ACTIVITY 2

他們在做甚麼？ What are they doing?

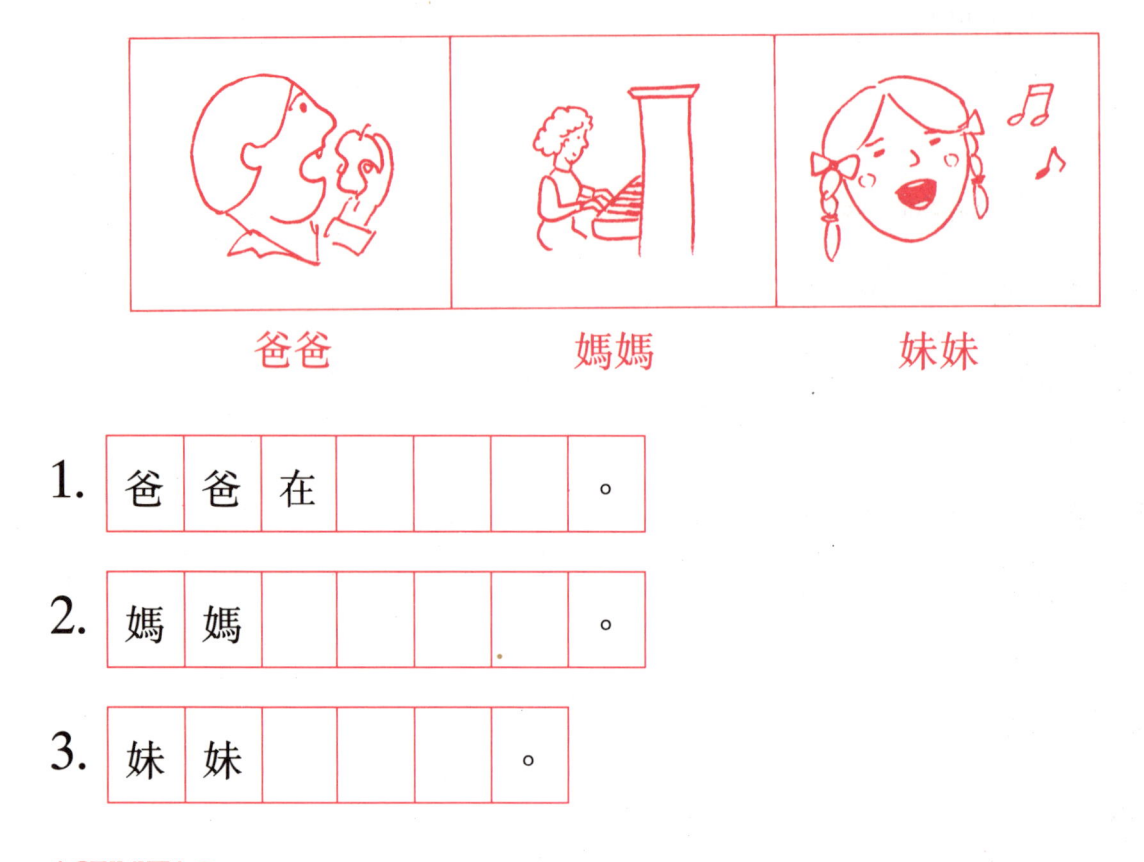

| 爸爸 | 媽媽 | 妹妹 |

1. | 爸 | 爸 | 在 | | | | 。 |

2. | 媽 | 媽 | | | | 。 |

3. | 妹 | 妹 | | | 。 |

ACTIVITY 3

Learn the following vocabulary first:

哪兒？	nǎer	náh yìh? na5 yi4	where?
巴士站	bā shì zhàn	bà sí jaahm ba1 si2 jaam6	bus stop
火車站	huǒ chē zhàn	fóu chè jaahm foh2 che1 jaam6	train station
郵政局	yóu zhèng jú	yàuh jing guhk yau4 jing3 guk6	Post Office
洗手間	xǐ shǒu jiān	sái sáu gàan sai2 sau2 gaan1	toilet

A foreigner is asking you for direction. Can you show him the direction where he should go?

e.g.

Foreigner: 巴士站在哪兒？

You: 巴 士 站 在 東 面 。

Foreigner: 火車站在哪兒？

You: ☐☐☐☐☐☐☐ 。

Foreigner: 郵政局在哪兒？

You: ☐☐☐☐☐☐☐ 。

Foreigner: 洗手間在哪兒？

You: ☐☐☐☐☐☐☐ 。

ACTIVITY 4

Riddle—answer the following questions.

1. 甚麼東西有紅的皮，可以吃？＿＿＿＿＿＿＿
2. 甚麼東西在中秋節吃的？＿＿＿＿＿＿＿
3. 甚麼雞不是雞？＿＿＿＿＿＿＿
4. 甚麼皮不受人歡迎？＿＿＿＿＿＿＿

ACTIVITY 5

What are these people doing?

      1   2   3

1. 他們在做甚麼？

| 他 | 們 | | | 。 |

2. 爸爸在做甚麼？

| 爸 | 爸 | | | 。 |

3. 陳小姐在做甚麼？

| 陳 | 小 | 姐 | | | 。 |

18 FILL IN THE FORM

掌握時間管理　提升生活方式

休息、工作再工作,現代城市人的生命似乎都要虛耗在繁忙的工作和生活雜務上。然而,日忙夜忙的生活方式是否代表我們有效地充份利用時間呢?答案當然不是。

要把忙亂的日子理順、享受和諧的生活節奏,掌握時間管理要訣最是要緊。Motorola "生活方式與時間管理座談會"就是特別為大家介紹這門學問而設。由時間管理專家介紹多項實用技巧,讓大家認識更有效的方式支配生活和時間。座談會歡迎公眾人士免費入場,惟座位有限,請從速報名訂座。

座談會地點:灣仔港灣道會議展覽中心408室

日期	時間	組別
94年12月17日	下午 2:00 - 3:30	□ 第一組 25-39歲在職婦女
	下午 4:30 - 6:00	□ 第二組 18-25歲青年男女
94年12月18日	下午 2:00 - 3:30	□ 第三組 25-39歲男女均可
	下午 4:30 - 6:00	□ 第四組 18-25歲青年男女

請在 □ 上加上 ✓ 號

報名請電:9663554 或
填妥下列報名表格
傳真至 9663599 即可。

"生活方式與時間管理" 座談會

姓名:＿＿＿＿＿＿＿＿＿＿＿＿＿＿

性別:＿＿＿＿＿＿＿　年齡:＿＿＿＿

電話:(公司)＿＿＿＿＿＿(住宅)＿＿＿＿

住址:＿＿＿＿＿＿＿＿＿＿＿＿＿＿
　　　＿＿＿＿＿＿＿＿＿＿＿＿＿＿

VOCABULARY

	Pinyin	Yale / Lau	English
掌握	zhǎngwò	jéung aàk / jeung² aak¹	control
時間	shíjiān	sih gaan / si⁶ gaan³	time
管理	guǎnlǐ	gún léih / goon² lei²	management
提升	tíshēng	tàih sìng / tai⁴ sing¹	lift up
生活	shēnghuó	sàng wuht / sang¹ wut⁶	life
方式	fàngshì	fòng sìk / fong¹ sik¹	style
姓名	xìngmíng	sing mìhng / sing³ ming⁴	name
性別	xìngbié	sing biht / sing³ bit⁶	sex
電話	diànhuà	dihn wá / din⁶ wa²	telephone
公司	gōngsī	gùng sì / gung¹ si¹	company
住宅	zhùzhái	jyuh jáak / jue⁶ jaak²	home, residence
年齡	niánlíng	nìhn lìhng / nin⁴ ling⁴	age
住址	zhùzhǐ	jyuh jí / jue⁶ ji²	address
座談會	zuòtánhuì	joh tàahm wúi / joh⁶ taam⁴ wooi²	conference (sit-talk meeting)

ADVERTISEMENT EXPLANATION

掌握時間管理，提升生活方式。

Pinyin: Zhǎngwò shíjiān guǎnlǐ, tíshēng shēnghuó fàngshì.
Yale: Jéung àk sih gaan gún leih, tàih sìng sàng wuht fòng sìk.
Lau: Jeung2 ak1 si6 gaan3 goon2 lei2, tai4 sing1 sang1 wut6 fong1 sik1.
English: Control (your) time management, lift up (your) life style.

ACTIVITY 1

Write the Chinese characters.

女 姓 夕 名

姓	名									

ｍ 雨 電 言 話

電	話									

亻 住 宀 宅

住	宅									

忄 性 尸 另 別

性	別									

八 公 刁 司

公	司									

ACTIVITY 2

Match the Chinese vocabulary with the pictures.

1. 姓名 •   • a. ♂♀

2. 性別 •   • b. Mary Chan

3. 電話 •   • c. ☎

4. 住址 •   • d. 21 years old

5. 年齡 •   • e. 19 C, Block A, Shatin Centre, Hong Kong

ACTIVITY 3

Form Filling—you are interested in the advertised conference. Fill in the following form for yourself.

"生活方式與時間管理" 座談會

姓名：＿＿＿＿＿＿＿＿＿＿＿＿＿＿＿＿＿＿＿＿＿＿

性別：＿＿＿＿＿＿＿＿＿＿　年齡：＿＿＿＿＿＿＿

電話：（公司）＿＿＿＿＿＿（住宅）＿＿＿＿＿＿

住址：＿＿＿＿＿＿＿＿＿＿＿＿＿＿＿＿＿＿＿＿＿＿

　　　＿＿＿＿＿＿＿＿＿＿＿＿＿＿＿＿＿＿＿＿＿＿

You have another friend who would like to join the conference too. Help him to fill in his form.

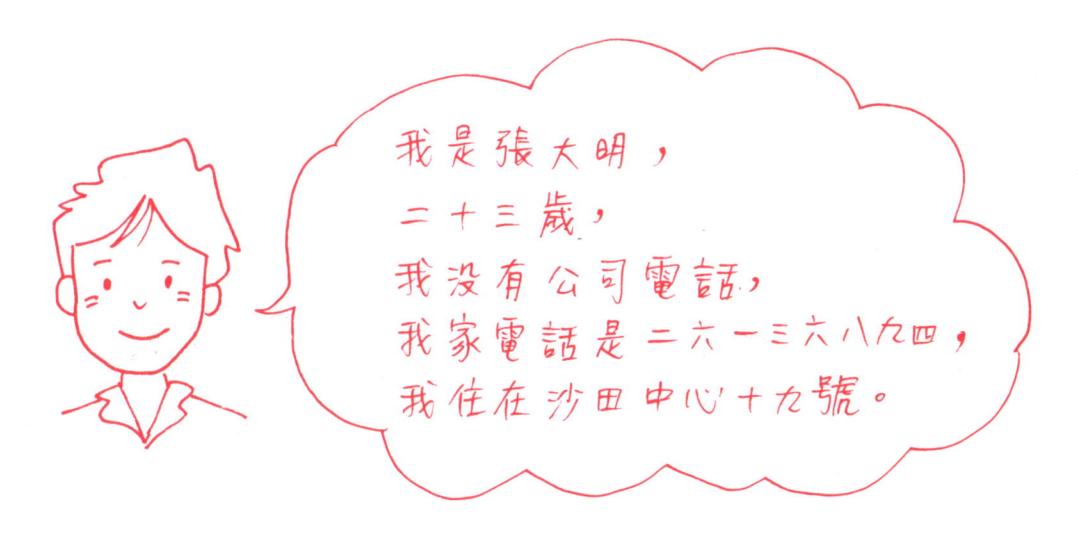

> 我是張大明，
> 二十三歲，
> 我沒有公司電話，
> 我家電話是二六一三六八九四，
> 我住在沙田中心十九號。

"生活方式與時間管理"座談會

姓名：＿＿＿＿＿＿＿＿＿＿＿＿＿＿＿＿＿＿＿＿＿＿＿＿＿＿

性別：＿＿＿＿＿＿＿＿＿＿＿＿ 年齡：＿＿＿＿＿＿＿＿

電話：（公司）＿＿＿＿＿＿＿＿（住宅）＿＿＿＿＿＿＿＿

住址：＿＿＿＿＿＿＿＿＿＿＿＿＿＿＿＿＿＿＿＿＿＿＿＿＿
＿＿＿＿＿＿＿＿＿＿＿＿＿＿＿＿＿＿＿＿＿＿＿＿＿＿＿＿

ACTIVITY 4

Domino game

To play the game, you have to cut the card that are enclosed at the end of book (entitled "unit 18"). The cards can be made into another set of 20 dominoes.
Play the game according to the same instruction as in unit 8.

ACTIVITY SHEET

UNIT 10

Activity 4—Ordering food in a Chinese restaurant.

Student B worksheet: you are pushing a dim sum trolley in a Chinese restaurant. You have the following dim sum in your trolley. Student A will ask you whether you have the dim sum he/she wants.

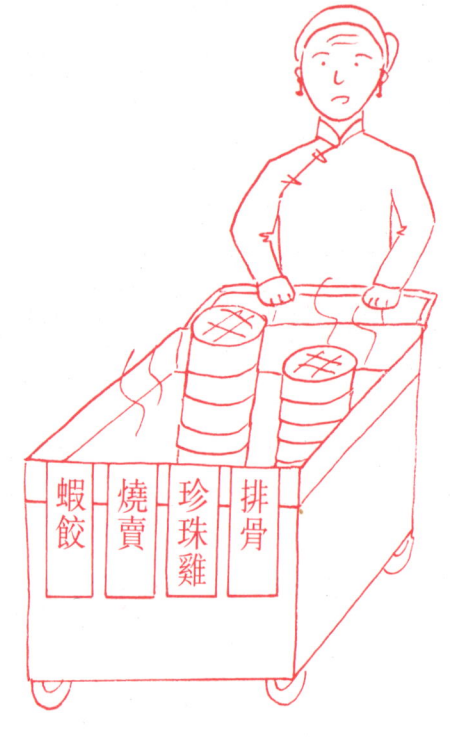

蝦餃　燒賣　珍珠雞　排骨

You may use these expressions to help you.

> customer: ……
>
> You: 有。我有……
>
> 　　　（對不起，我沒有……。）
>
> customer: ……

UNIT 11

Activity 2—Who is who?

Worksheet B: Here are six people and some information about them:

				18	

> Sally 最年輕。
>
> Bob 比 May 高但比 David 矮。
>
> May 比 Sally 和 Judy 肥。
>
> Judy 的頭髮比 Sally 的長。
>
> 最瘦的人是 16 歲。

Student A also has the information about the six people. Work together to see if you can work out their names and their ages. Write them in the boxes.

You are allowed to read out the information you have about the six people but you must not let student A see your book.

UNIT 14

Activity 4—Which one is the robber?

Student B: You are the witness of a robbery. You can still remember the robber's face. Tell the policeman what you saw when he/she asks you questions.

Witness

You can say 不知道 (bù zhī-dào, bàt jì dou, bat1 ji1 do3) if you don't know the answer.

UNIT 16

Activity 6—It is party time!

Student B worksheet: Listen to your parther's description and colour your mask accordingly.
Tell your partner the following description so that he/she can colour her/his mask according to your instruction.

藍色的頭髮。

黑色的眼。

白色的鼻子。

綠色的耳。

紅色的口。

ANSWER

UNIT 1

Activity 2: 1 c,   2 d,   3 f,   4 a,   5 e,   6 b
Activity 3: 1 最,   2 三角,   3 最
Activity 4: 1 False,   2 True,   3 False,   4 True

UNIT 2

Activity 2:

		五	
		土	二
	七		五
六	九		

Activity 3: 1 b,   2 a,   3 c,   4 e,   5 d
Activity 4: 1.
2.
3.

Activity 5: 1 杯   2 張   3 份   4 個   5 個

UNIT 3

Activity 2: 1 d   2 c   3 a   4 b
Activity 3: 1. 這杯茶很苦。   2. 這個橙很甜。
           3. 這個蘋果很好吃。   4. 我的橙很甜。
           5. 這本書最大。
Activity 4: 1. 這個蘋果很酸。   2. 這個蘋果很甜。
           3. 這個蘋果很好吃。   4. 這個蘋果最好吃。

UNIT 4

Activity 2:　　　　　　蘋果

　　　　　　　　　　吃蘋果

　　　　　　　　　想吃蘋果

　　　　　　　　媽媽想吃蘋果

　　　　　　　媽媽想我吃蘋果

　　　　　　媽媽想我吃蘋果，但我想吃橙。

Activity 3: 1 c,　2 a,　3 b,　4 d

UNIT 5

Activity 2: 甲有橙，乙有蘋果，丙有餅咭，丁有書。

Activity 3: 1 T,　2 T,　3 F,　4 F,　5 T

Activity 4: 1. 不是，2. 不是，3. 不是，4. 是

Activity 5: ② Amy,　③ Susan,　① Mary

UNIT 6

Activity 2: 1 b　2 a　3 d　4 e　5 c

Activity 3: 1 真長　2 真高　3 真好吃

Activity 4: roughly like this:

UNIT 7

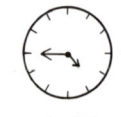

Activity 2: 1. 9:30　2. 6:00　3. 4:45　4. 8:35

Activity 3: 1 六時　2 五時半　3 吃　4 七時半

Activity 4: 1 e　2 d　3 c　4 a　5 b　6 f

UNIT 8

Activity 2: 1 b   2 a   3 d   4 c

UNIT 9

Activity 2: 1 c   2 d   3 e   4 a   5 b
Activity 3: 1 新年快樂！　2 聖誕快樂！　3 生日快樂！

UNIT 10

Activity 2: 1 c   2 a   3 b
Activity 3: 1 c   2 a   3 b   4 d

UNIT 11

Activity 2:

Sally	Judy	Bob	David	May	Joe
16	22	17	20	18	21

Activity 3: 從 A 到 B，從 B 到 C，從 C 到 E，從 E 到 F。時間：8 小時。

UNIT 12

Activity 2: 1. 來   2. 過來   3. 請過來   4. 老師，請過來
　　　　　　5. 老師，你可不可以過來？
Activity 3: 1 C   2 B   3 E   4 D   5 A

UNIT 13

Activity 2:

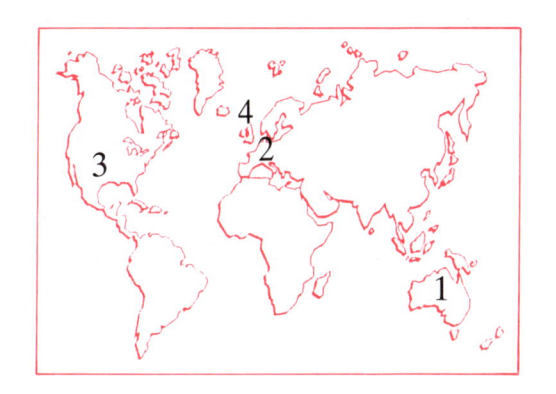

Activity 3: 1 英國人　2 美國人　3 法國人

Activity 4: 1. 可以　2. 不可以　3. 可以　4. 不可以

UNIT 14

Activity 2: 1 a　2 a　3 b　4 a

Activity 3: 1. 這書是你的嗎？　　2. 她是你的妹妹嗎？

　　　　　3. 你好嗎？

Activity 4: Number b

UNIT 15

Activity 2: 1. 不同　2. 不同　3. 相同　4. 不同　5. 不同

Activity 3: ☑ sing　☒ swim　☑ write Chinese　☒ make cakes

UNIT 16

Activity 2:　　　　百貨公司

　　　　　38 間百貨公司

　　　　全港 38 間百貨公司

　　　　全港 38 間百貨公司齊列。

　　　　全港 38 間百貨公司全部齊列。

Activity 3: 1. 不要開窗　2. 不要開燈　3. 不要開門

Activity 4: 1. 這全都是我的東西。（These are all mine.）

　　　　　2. 那全都是我的書。（Those are all my books.）

　　　　　3. 她們全都是我的朋友。（They are all my friends.）

Activity 5: 1 d　2 c　3 e　4 a　5 b

UNIT 17

Activity 2: 1. 吃蘋果　2. 在學鋼琴　3. 在唱歌

Activity 3: 火車站在北面。郵政局在南面。洗手間在西面。

Activity 4: 1. 蘋果　2. 月餅　3. 珍珠雞　4. 頭皮

Activity 5: 1. 在唱歌　2. 在看書　3. 在寫字。

UNIT 18

Activity 2: 1 b   2 a   3 c   4 e   5 d

Activity 3:

"生活方式與時間管理"座談會

姓名： 張大明

性別： 男   年齡： 23

電話：（公司） 沒有   （住宅） 26136894

住址： 沙田中心 19 號

VOCABULARY LIST

Vocabulary	Chinese	Simplified	Pinyin	Unit
a very happy surprise	喜出望外		xǐchū wàng wài	17
absolutely	絕對	绝对	juéduì	15
ache, pain	痛	疼	tòng	6
address	住址		zhùzhǐ	18
age	年齡	年龄	niánlíng	18
all, whole	全		quán	13, 16
all depend, reply on	全憑	全凭	quán píng	14
America	美國	美国	Měiguó	13
American	美國人	美国人	Měiguórén	13
and	並，和，與	并，和，与	bìng, hé, yǔ	9, 11
apple	蘋果	苹果	píngguǒ	2
at the same time	同時	同时	tóngshí	17
Australia	澳洲	沃洲	Àozhōu	13
Australian	澳洲人	沃洲人	Àonzhōurén	13
autumn	秋		qiū	8
beyond	超過	超过	chāo guò	11
big	大		dà	1

Vocabulary	Chinese	Simplified	Pinyin	Unit
birthday	生日		shēngrì	9
bitter	苦		kǔ	3
black	黑		hēi	16
blue	藍	蓝	lán	16
body	身體	身体	shēntǐ	9
bone	骨		gǔ	10
book	書	书	shū	2
bread, bun	飽	饱	bāo	10
bus stop	巴士站		bā shì zhàn	17
but	但		dàn	4
cake	餅	饼	bǐng	2
card	卡，咭		kǎ	2
care	關心	关心	guānxīn	12
carry	攜帶	携带	xiédài	14
celebrate	賀	贺	hè	9
chicken	雞	鸡	jī	10
chilli hot	辣		là	3
China	中國	中国	Zhōngguó	13
Chinese	中國人	中国人	Zhōngguórén	13
Chinese style	中式		zhōngshì	2

Vocabulary	Chinese	Simplified	Pinyin	Unit
chocolate	巧克力		qiǎo kè lì	1
choose	選擇	选择	xuǎnzé	4
Christmas	聖誕	圣诞	shèngdàn	9
circle, round	圓形	圆形	yuán xíng	1, 8
come	來	来	lái	12
company	公司		gōngsī	16, 18
complete, tidy	齊	齐	qí	16
completely	全面		quán miàn	14
conference	座談會	座谈会	zuòtán huì	18
convenient	方便		fāngbiàn	14
conversation	通話	通话	tōnghuà	14
country	國家	国家	guojiā	13
cow	牛		niú	10
cup	杯		be-i	2
dandruff	頭皮	头皮	tóupí	6
delicious	好吃		hǎo chī	3
department store	百貨公司	百货公司	bǎihuò gōngsī	16
different	不同		bùtóng	15
door	門	门	mén	16
down, below, bottom	下		xià	17

Vocabulary	Chinese	Simplified	Pinyin	Unit
dumplings	餃子	饺子	jiǎozi	10
ear	耳		ěr	6
east	東	东	dōng	17
easy	容易		róngyì	14
eat	吃		chī	3
eight	八		bā	2
elder brother	哥哥		gēge	4
elder sisiter	姐姐		jiějie	4
embarrasing	尷尬	尴尬	gānggà	6
England	英國	英国	Yīngguó	13
English, British	英國人	英国人	Yīngguórén	13
expect	期待		qīdài	11
eye	眼		yǎn	6
face (noun)	面		miàn	6
face (verb)	面對	面对	miàn duì	15
far	遠	远	yuǎn	11
fat	肥胖		féipàng	5
father	爸爸		bàba	4
fight	爭		zhēng	7
fish	魚		yú	10

125

Vocabulary	Chinese	Simplified	Pinyin	Unit
five	五		wǔ	2
four	四		sì	2
French	法國人	法国人	Fǎguó rén	13
friend	朋友		péngyǒu	2
from... to...	從…到…	从…到…	cóng… dào…	11
function	功能		gōngnéng	14
gift, present	禮物	礼物	lǐ wù	2
good thought	心意		xīnyì	2
green	綠	绿	lǜ	16
guest, client	客人		kèrén	15
hair	頭髮	头发	tóufà	6
happy	快樂	快乐	kuàilè	9
happy	喜		xǐ	17
have, has	有		yǒu	5
he, him	他		tā	2
head	頭	头	tóu	6
healthy	健康	健康	jiànkāng	9
heart	心		xīn	2
heavy	重		zhòng	5
her, hers	她，她的		tā, tāde	2

Vocabulary	Chinese	Simplified	Pinyin	Unit
here	這裏	这里	zhèli	16
hit, beat	打		dǎ	16
home	家		jiā	4
home, residence	住宅		zhùzhái	18
hour	時	时	shí	7
I, me	我		wǒ	2
imagine	想像	想象	xiǎngxiàng	11
itchy	痕		hěn	6
keep, store	收藏			
know at a glance	一望就知		yīwàng jiùzhī	14
lawyer	律師		lùshī	4
leaf	葉	叶	yè	10
learn	學	学	xué	4
life, living	生活		shēnghuó	18
lift up	提升		tíshēng	18
light, not heavy	輕	轻	qīng	5
list	列		liè	16
long	長	长	cháng	6, 14
look	望(看)		wàng (kàn)	17
lovers	情侶		qíng lǔ	1

127

Vocabulary	Chinese	Simplified	Pinyin	Unit
lucky	幸福		xìng fú	9
managment	管理		guǎnlǐ	18
many	多		duō	1
may, can, able to	可以		kěyi	13
merit	優點	优点	yōudiǎn	14
mid-autumn festival	中秋節	中秋节	zhōngqiūjié	8
middle, mid-	中		zhōng	8
minute(s)	分(分鐘)	分(分钟)	fēn (fēnzhōng)	7, 14
Miss, lady	小姐		xiǎojie	12
moon	月		yuè	8
moon cake	月餅	月饼	yuèbǐng	8
mother	媽媽	妈妈	māma	4
mouth	口(嘴)	口(咀)	kǒu (zǔi)	6
Mr., sir	先生		xiānshēng	12
Mrs., madam	太太		tàitai	12
must, should	必(一定)		bì (yī dìng)	7
my, mine	我的		wǒde	2
name	姓名		xīngmíng	18
never, cannot do	不會	不会	bùhuì	15
never mind	沒關係	沒关系	méi quānxi	11

Vocabulary	Chinese	Simplified	Pinyin	Unit
new	新		xīn	9
new year	新年		xīn nián	9
nice thought	心意		xīnyì	8
nine	九		jiǔ	2
north	北		běi	17
nose	鼻子		bízi	6
now	現在	现在	xiànzài	7
ocean	海洋		hǎiyáng	11
one	一		yī	2
only have, have nothing but	只得(只有)		zhǐde (zhǐyou)	14
only need	只需		zhǐxū	13
open	開		kāi	16
orange	橙		chéng	2
our, ours	我們的	我们的	wǒmende	2
out	出		chū	17
outside	外		wài	17
page	頁	页	yè	16
pass, send	傳	传	chuán	8
pearl	珍珠		zhēnzhū	10

Vocabulary	Chinese	Simplified	Pinyin	Unit
person, people	人		rén	2, 8
piano	鋼琴	钢琴	gāng qín	4
please	請	请	qǐng	12
popular	受歡迎	受欢迎	shòu huānyíng	1
Post Office	郵政局	邮政局	yóu zhèng jú	17
prawn	蝦	虾	xiā	10
prosperous, improve	進步	进步	jìnbù	9
quick, fast	快		kuài	7
real, really	真	真	zhēn	6
red	紅	红	hóng	16
relation	關係	关系	guān xi	1
result, outcome	結果	结果	jiéguǒ	14
same	相同		xiāngtóng	15
sea	海		hǎi	11
second	秒		miǎo	7
service	服務	服务	fúwù	16
seven	七		qī	2
sex	性別		xìngbié	18
she, her	她		tā	2

Vocabulary	Chinese	Simplified	Pinyin	Unit
short, not tall	矮		ǎi	5
short, not long	短		duǎn	6
show, depict	顯示	显示	xiǎnshì	14
sit	坐		zuò	13
six	六		liù	2
skin	皮		pí	6
sky	天空		tiānkōng	11
slow	慢		màn	7
small	小，細	小，细	xiǎo, xì	1, 14
sorry	對不起	对不起	duì bù qǐ	11
sour	酸		suān	3
south	南		nán	17
special	特別		tèbié	7
special delivery	專遞	专递	zhuándì	7
spring	春		chūn	8
sqaure	正方形		zhèng fāng xíng	1
stamp	郵票	邮票	yóupiào	13
stay	留		liú	4
study performance	學業	学业	xué yè	9
style	方式		fāngshì	18

Vocabulary	Chinese	Simplified	Pinyin	Unit
summer	夏		xià	8
sweet	甜		tián	3
swim	游泳		yóuyǒng	15
tall, high	高		gāo	3, 5
tea	茶		chá	2
teacher	老師		lǎo shī	4
telephone	電話	电话	diànhuà	18
ten	十		shí	2
thanks	謝謝	谢谢	xiè xie	11
the most	最		zuì	1
there	那裏	那里	nàli	16
they, them	他們	他们	tāmen	2
thin	瘦		shòu	5
thing, stuff	東西	东西	dōngxī	17
this	這	这	zhè	3
three	三		sān	2
time	時間	时间	shíjiān	7, 14, 18
toilet	洗手間	洗手间	xǐ shǒu jiān	17
too... (adj)	太		tài	5
tradition	傳統	传统	chuántǒng	2

Vocabulary	Chinese	Simplified	Pinyin	Unit
train station	火車站	火车站	huǒ chē zhàn	17
treat everyone equally	一視同仁	一视同仁	yīshìtóngrén	15
triangle	三角形		sānjiǎo xíng	1
two	二（兩）	两	èr (liǎng)	2, 8
united	團圓	团圆	tuányuán	8
up, on top	上		shàng	17
very	很		hěn	3
want	要		yào	4
we, us	我們	我们	wǒmen	2
wedding, married	結婚	结婚	jiéhūn	2
welcome	歡迎	欢迎	huān yíng	1
west	西		xī	17
what	甚（什）麼	什么	shénmó	7, 17
where	哪兒		nǎer	17
white	白		bái	16
who	誰	谁	shuí	12
wife	太太		tài tai	4
window	窗		chuāng	16
winter	冬		dōng	8

133

Vocabulary	Chinese	Simplified	Pinyin	Unit
wish, would like	想		xiǎng	4
within control	掌握		zhǎngwò	17, 18
word	字		zì	14
worm	蟲	虫	chóng	16
year	年		nián	9
years old	歲	岁	suì	11
yellow	黃	黄	huáng	16
you	你		nǐ	2, 5
you (pl.)	你們		nǐmen	2
young	年輕	年轻	niánqīng	11
younger brother	弟弟		dìdi	4
yougers sister	妹妹		mèimei	4
your, yours	你的		nǐde	2

SIMPLIFIED VOCABULARY LIST

UNIT 1

歡迎 ⟷ 欢迎

關係 ⟷ 关系

圓形 ⟷ 圆形

UNIT 2

結婚 ⟷ 结婚

餅咭 ⟷ 饼咭

傳統 ⟷ 传统

禮物 ⟷ 礼物

蘋果 ⟷ 苹果

書 ⟷ 书

我們 ⟷ 我们

個 ⟷ 个

隻 ⟷ 只

UNIT 3

這 ⟷ 这

UNIT 4

媽媽 ⟷ 妈妈

學 ⟷ 学

鋼琴 ⟷ 钢琴

老師 ⟷ 老师

選擇 ⟷ 选择

UNIT 5

輕 ⟷ 轻

UNIT 6

頭 ⟷ 头

頭皮 ⟷ 头皮

尷尬 ⟷ 尴尬

頭髮 ⟷ 头发

痛 ⟷ 疼

長 ⟷ 长

UNIT 7

專遞 ⟷ 专递

時 ⟷ 时

時間 ⟷ 时间

現在 ⟷ 现在

甚麼 ⟷ 什么

UNIT 8

傳 ←→ 传
兩 ←→ 两
團圓 ←→ 团圆
月餅 ←→ 月饼
中秋節 ←→ 中秋节

UNIT 9

聖誕 ←→ 圣诞
快樂 ←→ 快乐
進步 ←→ 进步
身體 ←→ 身体
健康 ←→ 健康
學業 ←→ 学业
並賀 ←→ 并贺

UNIT 10

餃子 ←→ 饺子
蝦餃 ←→ 虾饺
燒賣 ←→ 烧卖
飽 ←→ 饱
鳳爪 ←→ 凤爪
牛栢(柏)葉 ←→ 牛柏叶

雞 ←→ 鸡
謝 ←→ 谢
對不起 ←→ 对不起
請問 ←→ 请问
關係 ←→ 关系

UNIT 11

榮 ←→ 荣
遠 ←→ 远
超過 ←→ 超过
想像 ←→ 想象
三歲 ←→ 三岁
年輕 ←→ 年轻
從 ←→ 从
與 ←→ 与

UNIT 12

誰 ←→ 谁
來 ←→ 来
關心 ←→ 关心
陳太太 ←→ 陈太太
過來 ←→ 过来
請 ←→ 请

UNIT 13

郵票	←→	邮票
國	←→	国
一個	←→	一个
澳洲	←→	沃洲

UNIT 14

分鐘	←→	分钟
通話	←→	通话
時間	←→	时间
優點	←→	优点
攜帶	←→	携带
全憑	←→	全凭
顯示	←→	显示
結果	←→	结果
細小	←→	细小

UNIT 15

面對	←→	面对
絕對	←→	绝对
不會	←→	不会
一視同仁	←→	一视同仁

UNIT 16

蟲	←→	虫
開	←→	开
黃頁	←→	黄页
服務	←→	服务
齊	←→	齐
紅	←→	红
綠	←→	绿
藍	←→	蓝
門	←→	门
窗	←→	窗
百貨	←→	百货
這裏	←→	这里
裏	←→	里
圖	←→	图
類	←→	类

UNIT 17

甚麼	←→	什么
東西	←→	东西
同時	←→	同时

火車站	⟷	火车站
郵政局	⟷	邮政局
洗手間	⟷	洗手间

UNIT 18

時間	⟷	时间
電話	⟷	电话
年齡	⟷	年龄
座談會	⟷	座谈会

Domino game   Unit 8

△	辣	M+M	瘦
○	三角形	☽	朱古力（巧克力）
□	圓形	鼻	月
♡	正方形	口	鼻
檸檬	心	耳	口
糖	酸	眼	耳
門	甜	頭	眼
人們	高	髮	頭
矮人	矮	臉	頭髮
肥人	肥	辣椒	面

P : shào
Y : sau
L : sau³

P : qiǎo kè lì
Y : jyù gù lìk
L : jue¹ gwoo lik¹

P : yuè
Y : yuht
L : yut⁶

P : bízu
Y : beih
L : bei⁶

P : kǒu
Y : háu
L : hau²

P : ěr
Y : yíh
L : yi⁵

P : yǎn
Y : ngáahn
L : ngaan⁵

P : tóu
Y : tàuh
L : tau⁴

P : tóu fà
Y : tàuh faat
L : tau⁴ faat³

P : miàn
Y : mihn
L : min⁶

P : là
Y : laaht
L : laat⁶

P : sān jiǎo xíng
Y : sàam gok yìhng
L : saam¹ gok³ ying⁴

P : yuán xíng
Y : yùhn yìhng
L : yuen⁴ ying⁴

P : zhèng fāng xíng
Y : jing fòng yìhng
L : jing³ fong¹ ying⁴

P : xīng
Y : sàm
L : sam¹

P : suān
Y : sỳun
L : suen¹

P : tián
Y : tìhm
L : tim⁴

P : gāo
Y : gòu
L : go¹

P : ǎi
Y : ái
L : ai²

P : féi
Y : fèih
L : fei⁴

Unit 18

🍎	書	🦐	魚
🍊	蘋果	🐛	蝦
☕	橙	🏛 (stamp)	蟲
🎁	杯	👤	郵票
🍰	禮物	☎	人
🎹	餅	Name:	電話
🦘	鋼琴	19C, Block A Shatin Centre Hong Kong	姓名
🐄	澳洲	🗽	住址
🐔	牛	🗼	美國
🐟	雞	📖	法國

P : yǔ
Y : yùh
L : yue⁴

P : xiā
Y : hà
L : ha¹

P : chońg
Y : chùhng
L : chung⁴

P : yóu piào
Y : yàuh piu
L : yau⁴ piu³

P : rén
Y : yàhn
L : yan⁴

P : diàn huà
Y : dihn wá
L : din⁶ wa²

P : xìng míng
Y : sing mīhng
L : sing³ ming⁴

P : zhù zhǐ
Y : jyuh jí
L : jue⁶ ji²

P : Měi guó
Y : Méi gwok
L : Mei² gwok³

P : Fǎ guó
Y : Faat gwok
L : Faat³ gwok³

P : shū
Y : syù
L : sue¹

P : píng guǒ
Y : pìhng gwó
L : ping⁴ gwo²

P : chéng
Y : cháang
L : chaang²

P : bèi
Y : bùi
L : bui¹

P : lǐ wù
Y : láih maht
L : lai⁵ mat⁶

P : bǐng
Y : béng
L : beng²

P : gāng gín
Y : gong kàhm
L : gong³ 'kam⁴

P : Ào zhōu
Y : Ou jàu
L : Ou³ jau¹

P : niú
Y : ngàuh
L : ngau⁴

P : jī
Y : gài
L : gai¹